THE EFFECTIVENESS OF CAUSES

Causation is one of the perpetual problems of philosophy. In her latest book Dorothy Emmet starts from the obvious point that causes need effects, and says that some prevalent views fail to account for the *effectiveness* of causes. These views take causes and effects to be events which are instances of laws. This may do for one kind of causal *explanation*, but not for a metaphysics of the world in which causal relations are supposed to hold. It only gives a world of events, each of which is presented as an unchanging unit. She calls such a world a 'Zeno universe', since in it transitions (and in the end movement) get lost. Since she thinks the world is not like this, she locates causation not in events but in their 'participants'. Thus construed, so-called event causation is just one kind of 'transeunt' causation, where effects succeed their causes in time. But there is also 'immanent' causation, where the effects are not temporally separable from their causes. Dorothy Emmet sees immanent causation in the mere fact that anything persists, in certain organic and mental processes, and perhaps in the operation of what is called 'efficacious grace'. Thus the notion of Cause is not a single nor a simple one. In general it stands for there being something on which something else depends; but causal dependence can take various forms, some of which call for a strong view which has implications for other metaphysical questions.

Dorothy Emmet is Professor Emeritus of Philosophy of the University of Manchester. She read Greats at Lady Margaret Hall, Oxford, worked for two winters as a tutor at the Maesyrhaf Educational Settlement in the Rhondda Valley, and held a Commonwealth Fellowship at Radcliffe College, Cambridge, Mass., where she studied with A. N. Whitehead. From 1932 to 1938 she was Lecturer in Philosophy at King's College, Newcastle upon Tyne, and went from there to the University of Manchester, first as Lecturer in the Philosophy of Religion and then as Sir Samuel Hall Professor of Philosophy. She is now retired and living in Cambridge.

She is the author of *Whitehead's Philosophy of Organism*, *The Nature of Metaphysical Thinking*, *Function, Purpose and Powers*, *Rules, Roles and Relations*, and *The Moral Prism*, and co-editor (with Alistair MacIntyre) of *Sociological Theory and Philosophical Analysis*.

SUNY Series in Philosophy
Robert C. Neville, Editor

THE EFFECTIVENESS OF CAUSES

Dorothy Emmet

State University of New York Press
Albany

First published in U.S.A. by
State University of New York Press, Albany

For information, address State University of New York Press,
State University Plaza, Albany, N.Y., 12246

Printed in Hong Kong

Library of Congress Cataloging in Publication Data

Emmet, Dorothy Mary, 1904–
The effectiveness of causes.

(SUNY series in philosophy)
Bibliography: p.
Includes index.
1. Causation. 2. Act (Philosophy) I. Title.
II. Series.
BD591.E48 1984   122   84–5616
ISBN 0–87395–940–X
ISBN 0–87395–941–8 (pbk.)

Contents

To R. B. Braithwaite

Preface

This is a monograph, not a comprehensive discussion of Causation. It divides roughly into two halves. In Chapters 1–7, I work towards what I want to say, taking account of some contemporary views. Here my main indebtedness is to the writings of Donald Davidson, in spite of disagreements which will be apparent. In Chapters 8–11 I become increasingly metaphysical, Here my references are apt to be to philosophers of an older generation. I had not noticed that there was this distinction until it was pointed out to me by Frederick Schick. It is not just due to the accident that they happened to be the philosophers who were writing when I came in. These older philosophers were more concerned than our contemporaries with the underlying questions of what the world needed to be like to sustain their views on causation. And there is always Aristotle, who came in before any of us, and who appears in both parts.

One of the older philosophers on whom I draw in the second part is A. N. Whitehead. My early work in philosophy was sparked off by reading him in the 1920s. I now find myself distanced from his later writings, but increasingly sympathetic to the middle ones, especially when he was working towards a generalised notion of 'organism', and when his 'passage of nature' could be seen not as one damn thing after another, but as a pattern-forming and pattern-sustaining process which could support a dynamic view of a causation underlying more restricted kinds. I have to thank Margaret Masterman for encouraging me to look again at *The Concept of Nature* with this in mind.

Some people have claimed to find a difference of meaning between 'causation' and 'causality'. This seems to me purely stipulative, and I do not think it matters which form one uses so long as one sticks to it. I have chosen 'causation', but of course when I am quoting people who say 'causality' I follow their usage.

Frederick Schick read a complete draft, and gave me valuable advice, particularly on the structuring. Jeremy Butterfield, Jane Heal and Anthony Appiah have helped me by their comments. I owe a great deal to

vii

discussions with Hugh Mellor. The dedication to R. B. Braithwaite is a mark of affection and gratitude for what he has given me in talks about philosophy on many occasions. Of course none of these friends is committed to any agreement with my views. I also want to thank Joyce Burkinshaw for her skilful typing and Gladys Keable for reading the proofs.

Finally, I salute the people who discover causes, and do not only write about causation: '*Felix qui potuit rerum cognoscere causas.*'

Cambridge   DOROTHY EMMET

Acknowledgements

The author and publishers wish to thank the following, who have kindly given permission for the use of copyright material:

William Heinemann Ltd for the extract from *Wind, Sand and Stars* by Antoine de Saint-Exupéry.

Institute for the Study and Treatment of Delinquency for the extract from the article 'Unscientific, Unwise, Unprofitable and Unjust' by Nigel Walker, in the *British Journal of Criminology*, vol. 22, no. 3, July 1982.

Oxford University Press for the extracts from *Essays on Actions and Events* by D. Davidson; *Philosophical Papers* by J. L. Austin, and *Collected Letters of S. T. Coleridge*, vol. V.

Routledge & Kegan Paul Ltd for the extracts from *Actions* by J. Hornsby.

1 Introduction

When we ask why something happens or has happened, from earthquakes to car accidents or urban riots, we ask for its cause or causes. 'Cause' comes into practical life, into the experimental sciences, and, perhaps more controversially, into scientific theories. We constantly use it; and yet when we start thinking about what it means, it becomes increasingly problematic. And when pressed, these problems are likely to take us from practical uses through scientific uses into metaphysics. There is a vast literature on all this: it concentrates attention on the notion of cause, but less, it seems to me, on the notion of *effect*. Yet cause and effect are correlative; a cause is supposed to have an effect, to be efficacious.

The quick comment might be that of course we believe in effects; otherwise why should we look for causes, whether in everyday life or in the sciences. So causes are efficacious, genuinely *effective*. I believe that this quick comment is in fact the right one: but its justification is not obvious and can be challenged.

It can be challenged because it is not clear what such 'efficacy' consists in. It is said to be the relic of an anthropomorphic view of the world, in which forces in nature are thought of as pushing and pulling and making things happen because we ourselves push and pull and make things happen. So to believe in natural efficacy is an animistic superstition.

The charge of 'superstition', may not only refer to supposed animism. There is a remark of Wittgenstein's 'Belief in the causal nexus is superstition' – '*Der Glaube an der Kausalnexus ist der Aberglaube*' (*Tractatus Logico-Philosophicus* 5. 1361), on which Waismann is reported to have commented '*Aberglaube – aber Glaube*' – superstition, but (nevertheless) belief.[1] Wittgenstein was, I think, referring not so much to the 'anthropomorphic' analogy as to the view that one event called a cause *entails* its effect, so that belief in the causal nexus allows inference from one state of affairs to another. Inference is a logical relationship – connections described by cause and effect are not logical connections, but empirically observed sequences. When similar sequen-

1

ces are found repeatedly, they can be called causal sequences. Hume said this; necessary connections belong to logic, and no one can *perceive* a logical necessary connection between states of affairs. What we perceive are sequences of states of affairs, with repeated properties, and we then generalise about these repetitions and expect these repetitions to be continued in the future. Latter-day Humeans have considerably sophisticated this view; for instance they put the sequences within wider settings to distinguish them from coincidences, but they still give us sequences in which events or states of affairs called causes have successors, and though these may be called 'effects' they are not in any strong sense something *effected*. We may want to go further than this: to have causes with real efficacy to produce real effects; and say that the 'successor' view does not take us as far as we want to go.

It might be said that whether or not the sequential view is as far as we *want* to go, it is as far as we *can* go, unless we are to leave what is reasonably objective and supported by observation for what is subjective and speculative. If we go further and bring some kind of productivity into our account, this can be called 'anthropomorphic superstition'.

If a view is anthropomorphic, then at least it ought to be proper to use it of human beings. So if saying that causation is an actual production of effects is anthropomorphic, at any rate we shall need to see how this may properly apply in the case of the *anthropos*. The 'superstition' would then consist in extending it beyond the human world. The *locus classicus* for this view was Kelsen's *Society and Nature*.[2] Human beings find that they have power to make things happen; they then see causation as a matter of powers in nature making things happen. Moreover, human beings are responsible for the results of their actions, and what they can do (in one sense of 'can') is set out in moral laws. Then primitive and also Greek notions of Law in the physical world are said to be thought of in analogy to moral norms, so that 'transgressing' them brings retribution. Also in early Greek philosophy there is 'Ανάγκη, Necessity, a power which keeps nature in its due course – and if things do not keep their due course, the *Erinyes*, the Furies, as agents of Zeus, will pursue them. This is to see natural laws as causal laws, and causes as like agents having responsibility for their effects. (Note that in Greek αἰτία means both cause and guilt.)[3]

I am not at all convinced that 'primitive' people or the Greeks only thought of causation on the model of human agency. Contemporary anthropologists, such as Evans-Pritchard and Max Gluckman, report that in some cases where ill ensues for the people concerned there is a belief in a double causation.[4] Your hut falls down because termites have eaten the bases of its supports. But why should they have attacked *your* hut and not the next man's, or, better still, a tree at a safe distance? Witchcraft must have directed them – a cause commensurable in power with the seriousness of the damage, and of malignant intent – otherwise how answer the question 'Why should this happen to *me*?' At the same time, the fact that termites eating away supports will cause them to collapse is perfectly well understood – it is the particular incidence of this in befalling a particular person which needs further explanation.

Nevertheless, the termites did something when they ate away the supports. So the cause may be seen as some kind of agency, though not a personal one. Where the agency is personal, $αἰτία$ as guilt may be imputed. If it is not personal, $αἰτία$ as guilt may pass over into being $αἰτία$ as cause, shedding the ascription of responsibility.[5] Nevertheless, the notion of agency in $αἰτία$ as cause may still be a ghost of the notion of human agency. This has been well said by J. L. Austin:

> 'Causing', I suppose, was a notion taken from a man's own experience of doing simple actions, and by primitive man every event was construed in terms of this model: every event has a cause, that is, every event is an action done by somebody – if not by a man, then by a quasi-man, a spirit. When, later, events which are *not* actions are realized to be such, we still say that they must be 'caused', and the word snares us: we are struggling to ascribe to it a new, unanthropomorphic meaning, yet constantly, in searching for its analysis, we unearth and incorporate the lineaments of the ancient model. As happened even to Hume, and consequently to Kant. Examining such a word historically, we may well find that it has been extended to cases that have by now too tenuous a relation to the model case, that it is a source of confusion and superstition.[6]

So, Austin says, the word 'cause' snares us; 'we are struggling to ascribe to it a new, unanthropomorphic meaning, yet constantly, in searching for its analysis, we unearth and incorporate the lineaments of the ancient model'.

Humeans, past and present, struggle to resist this. They may not only struggle; they may legislate, not only for us, but for the notion itself. So A. R. White, referring to those who hold that 'because', when it gives a reason for an action, cannot be giving a cause, says that for something to qualify as a cause 'it must observe Hume's rule'.[7] We are not told what sanctions would be applied if 'cause' refuses to observe the rule. However, even some of those who would like to see it complying have a feeling that the rule may be too restrictive. There may be more to cause and effect than regular succession, even succession within a context of wider theory. But what more? Those who feel this way may just note that there is probably more to be said, and then pass on. So Donald Davidson, to whose views on the logic of causal statements I shall be returning, says that it is the *logic of causal statements* and not the causal relation itself with which he is concerned; the discussion of the latter is something which, at any rate at this stage, he has 'abjured'.[8] D. H. Mellor in his recent book *Real Time* uses the notion of causation to give the basic relation of 'earlier than' and 'later than'; he then takes causation as that which (*inter alia*) makes it more and less likely that something which has a property at one time will have the same or a different property at another time, and goes on to say 'What else causation needs, besides this causal sort of probability and the correlation that reveals it, is also debatable, although it clearly needs something. But besides the assumptions I have already made, I can and will keep out of the debate.'[9] J. L. Mackie, in his book *The Cement of the Universe* (Hume's phrase for what causation is *to us* – Hume's italics – as one of the 'ties of our thoughts'), concludes that 'the universe needs to know where to go next'[10] – a riddling enough remark for one of the abjurors of anthropomorphism. He uses it as 'suggesting that there is some truth in the notion that what happens next *flows from* what is there already'. But this points to metaphysical questions which he does not pursue. Finally in our sample, Richard Taylor, who has written extensively on Cause, and who takes a stronger view than most of his contemporaries, leaves us with the dispiriting conclusion that:

> to say that A made B happen obviously only means that A *caused* B, and to say that it did this by virtue of its power to do so obviously means nothing more than that A produced B by virtue of its efficacy as a *cause* – or, in short, that A caused B. To say of anything, then, that it was the cause of something else, means simply and solely that it *was* the cause of the thing in question, and there is absolutely no other conceptually clearer way of putting the matter except by the introduction of mere synonyms for causation. Positively, what this means is that causation is a philosophical category, that while the concept of causation can perhaps be used to shed light upon other problems or used in the analysis of other relationships, no other concepts can be used to analyze it.[11]

Nevertheless, a very large number of philosophers have not been content, and still are not content, to accept this 'No Entry' sign. My excuse for beating at the barrier is perhaps in the end the only excuse in philosophy: a persistent worry. But further to this, I have a hope that if one can get beyond the discussion of the logic and epistemology of causal statements and get into the ontology underlying them, this may lead into an approach to certain metaphysical questions which do not go away. And this is why I am writing about causation.

Roughly, I see a cause as something on which something happening to something else depends. The dependence is not a logical one, and it can take more than one form. Whatever the form, the change which is the effect is not just *post hoc* but *propter hoc*; the cause is effective.

2 Causation in a Zeno Universe

Causation is generally thought to be a relation between two units, one the cause, the other the effect. Since Hume's attack on necessary connection, philosophers have been very aware of a problem about what kind of a relation this is. They have been less concerned over what are the kinds of unit between which the relation is supposed to hold. There are various candidates, of which a short list would contain facts, states of affairs, properties, events, and in contemporary discussions the preferred candidate has been events.

What then, are 'events'? We can start by saying an event is a happening with a spatio–temporal location. Your marriage is an event, an eruption of Etna is an event, Italy winning the World Cup is an event. Often an event is a change in a person, as would be your marriage, or in a thing, as would be an eruption of Etna; the winning of the World Cup is not primarily a change in persons (though it no doubt has considerable effects on the winners and losers), or in a thing (though the bit of hardware which is the actual cup may change its location). The winning of the World Cup is more like an achievement producing a change of status within the institutionalised setting of 'sporting events'. The creation of a positron and an electron could be an event, but not a change, since there was no already existing thing to change (even if the electron can be called a thing, which is doubtful).[1]

Events as we name them and think about them are events under descriptions. A description picks out an event in a phrase – the erupting of Etna, the spilling of my coffee. The former can be serious in its effects, the latter trivial; so an event to be picked out need not be all that noteworthy. But to be picked out at all, it must be of some interest in some context.

> Say not 'a small event!.' Why 'small'?
> Costs it more pain that this ye call

6

A 'great event' should come to pass
Than that?

says Browning in 'Pippa Passes'. But note that the 'small event' cost pain, and this was sufficient to mark it out. There are, of course, innumerable happenings at any given time; not only what Coleridge called 'all the numberless goings-on of life',[2] but all the numberless goings-on of nature, including those in outer space. We describe such goings-on as are relevant to an interest in hand. Sometimes of course a garrulous talker overdoes the circumstantial detail in recounting events, and this becomes boring; in some cases he may have to be asked to confine himself to what is relevant. If the policeman says 'Describe the events leading up to the accident', he will not thank you if you say you were walking along the road, and you put one foot forward, and then the other foot forward, and then the first foot . . . , and you say that a bird was singing in a tree . . . and so on (there might however be another story in which these events – though not others – would properly be included). If we had no interest in anything that was happening, and nothing bore on any of our purposes, we might say we had spent an uneventful afternoon.[3]

I should not want to try to clinch a discussion of what events are by appealing to how we talk about them in ordinary and practical contexts. However, how we talk in such contexts points to a feature which is, I think, important when trying to see what sort of 'ontological status' they may have (and above all what their role is in causal statements). This feature is their being selected from a background and we can only speak of them as edited under descriptions.[4] The form of the description can vary; I am sympathetic to what is called a gerundial nominalisation – 'the sinking of the Titanic', 'the slamming of the door', rather than a propositional factual statement – 'that the Titanic sank', 'that the door slammed'. I prefer the former, because, as 'nominalisations', they are less like propositions, and as '*verb* nominalisations' they retain a suggestion of a happening rather than of a thing.

Where causation is seen as a relation between events, these will also normally be seen as forming a contiguous sequence. We may indeed select some member of the chain not immediately contiguous with the effect and call it the cause, in accordance with some particular diagnostic interest. Nevertheless, we normally think that there will be other members leading from this one to a member spatially and temporally contiguous with the effect.[5] Contiguity is not the same as continuity, which can be defined mathematically by saying that between any two points another point can be inserted. In contiguity two things or segments are juxtaposed so that there is no gap between them. This can mean that they have a common boundary. They are distinguishable, but need not be discrete.

Contiguity is generally thought of spatially, rather than as immediate temporal antecedence, but in talk about causation it is likely to be spoken of as both spatial and temporal. One such view is Ducasse's.[6] For Ducasse, causes and effects are events. Causes and effects are events as changes in objects, and the cause of a particular change, K, is that event, C, which alone occurred in the immediate environment of K immediately before the change; and this is observable in the singular case. Causes and effects occur in time segments, and there must be a cut between the segment in which the cause occurs and the segment in which the effect occurs. There are two difficulties here; how do we know that there is only *one* event occurring in the immediate environment before the event called the effect; and if, as Ducasse says, the cut between these is a cut between segments in time, how does a cut in the time sequence answer to a cut between an event to be called a cause and an event to be called an effect, beyond saying that one precedes the other? His answer to the first question is that if there is more than one change in the immediate environment, then the change that immediately preceded that event is complex. A change can be single without being simple. But this does not meet the possibility that there may be a vast number of changes going on in the immediate environment. The question of which one to select and test as cause is not just settled by proximity, though changes in the proximate environment may suggest what factors to look at. 'Environment' is of course a spatial notion, whereas 'immediate antecedent' is a temporal one. If the cuts are between the time segments, there needs to be a way of deciding that a cut corresponds to the distinction between cause and effect. The segments will therefore have to be more than just segments in time.

One answer is that where the segments are seen as events, they display properties over and above spatio–temporal ones. If one event could only be distinguished from another by location in space–time, we might talk about different regions, but hardly about different events. An event is something occurring in a place at a time, and it can be described in a 'nominalisation', a phrase in which a noun is obtained from a verb: 'the ringing of the bells'. This event can be bounded by other events, 'the bells beginning to ring' and 'the bells stopping ringing'. All of these events happen or they do not; they may be changes (no pun about bell ringing intended) but they themselves are said not to change. Change can simply be the fact that an event at time T_1 has different properties from an event at time T_2. (Or we could say the event at T_2 marks a change in some object O as having different properties at T_2 from those it had at T_1. Here, however, I am speaking of changes as seen in terms of events.) When a change is said to be caused, it should be possible to predict some property or properties of an event E_2 at T_2 from those of an event E_1 at T_1. Then E_1 and and E_2 should form a sequence which can be compared with other sequences and connected with a generalisation supporting the prediction. Such a distinguishable sequence of events is, I think, what Russell means by a 'causal line'.[7]

The events have properties which resemble each other or differ in a predictable way along the causal line. So events are characterised by properties, and each event is described through its properties. If we have an ontology of events (as I think Russell does in the passage referred to), a change will not be something happening in a changing thing, but a difference between the properties of one event and those of another succeeding event. The events themselves do not change; they have whatever properties they have, and causation is invoked to predict these properties with the help of background generalisations.

We have an event E with properties pqz at time t and another event E_1 with properties $p_1 q_1 z_1$ at time t_1 and another, E_2, with properties $p_2 q_2 r_2$ at t_2. These can be arranged in a sequence:

E with pqz at t	E_1 with $p_1 q_1 r_1$ at t_1	E_2 with $p_2 q_2 r_2$ at t_2

and so on. The sequence can be predictable and there can be, but need not be, a common boundary of E and E_1 and of E_1 and E_2. Where there is, they can be said to be contiguous. But since the events are what they are, E does not pass into E_1 or E_1 into E_2. They form a sequence, but there is no transition, in the sense of a real movement from the one to the other. I call this kind of event ontology that of a Zeno universe; Zeno's arrow occupied a series of positions, but these gave no movement from one to the other:

(I am, of course, only referring here to Zeno's paradox of the Moving Arrow. His other paradoxes, notably that of Achilles and the Tortoise, about how a finite interval can contain an infinite number of intervals, are putting a different problem.) Russell's view of motion in *The Principles of Mathematics*[8] is, I would claim, a Zeno view. Motion is defined as the occupation by one entity of a continuous series of places at a continuous series of times. 'Change is the difference, in respect of truth and falsehood, between a proposition concerning an entity at time T and a proposition concerning the same entity at another time T_1, provided that the two propositions differ only by the fact that T occurs in the one where T_1 occurs in the other. Change is continuous when the propositions form a continuous series correlated with a continuous series of moments.' Motion consists in the correlation of the occupation of places and times, when different times are correlated with different places and are continuous. (Continuity would here mean that between any two places or times there can be a further one). I call this a Zeno view because motion is so defined as to lose transition. There is a mathematical treatment of continuity, but no transition.

I shall be claiming that an adequate view of causation will have to show change as involving transition, and not only change as defined as difference of properties at different times. It will need to be a view not only of an *eventum* which is the outcome of the change, but of an *eveniens*, which is the happening of one.

Intuitively we are aware of movements and transitions, and this, I believe, is a primitive experience. In order to get these into the account of causal relations the emphasis may be put not on events themselves, but on our perceptions of events. Michotte claimed to do this in what he called 'the perception of causality'.[9] He gives a phenomenology of what subjects report they see in what they describe as causal processes. What they see are two ways in which one movement seems to be continued into another. The first he calls 'launching', where one movement is seen as setting off another. The other is 'entraining' where the movement of one is seen as continuing in the movement of another (as when one truck runs into the back of another and they both continue together).[10] Michotte's claim is that people see these continuities; they do not, as Hume would have it, perceive them as distinct existences. And *one* perception is enough for them to make the report; there do not have to be repetitions in which they see similar sequences.

Is this really a perception of *causation*, or is it a report of what look like continuous processes with different stages? In fact, Michotte's apparently continuous movements may not actually be so. In some of his experiments he produced a cinematograph effect of continuity of movement by showing coloured strips through slits in moving discs, producing the illusion of one 'causing the movement in another'. So someone he calls a discerning colleague is quoted as saying 'What it amounts to is this. You start off with an illusion, and use it to prove that causal impressions are real and objective'[11], and Michotte rejoins that this is just what he does claim; but nevertheless the fact that we can act in ways adapted to our environment shows that generally speaking there is a wide correspondence between our phenomenal experience of seeing continuous processes, and what is happening in the physical world.

Be that as it may, what Michotte is talking about are visual perceptions of continuous movement which are interpreted by the kinetics of moving objects in space; the fact that we have such perceptions indicates that we live in a world where one movement gets continued into another. Michotte makes it easier to call this a perception of *causality* by dividing the continuous movement into two movements, one being that of the 'agent' and the other of the 'patient', and he can do this because what is perceived is not only movement but moving *objects*, for example a truck continuing to move forward and carrying another truck along with it. So what is reported as perceived is not just continuity of movement, but movement in one object as continuous with movement in another; however, this perceived continuity of movement can be an illusion, as in the cinema. Michotte has not therefore shown that our perception of movement is in fact a perception of causality. The perception of movement gives succession, but the movement may be being simulated through a succession of stills, as in a film.[12] However, in either case what we perceive comes in an order. Even if the film were run backwards, the movements which we were perceiving would come in an order which could not be reversed just by altering the order in which we looked.

Kant took Cause to be the category we apply to a succession of perceptions which we find to be irreversible in the temporal order in which we perceive them. Successions of perceptions can be reversible, as when we perceive a house from top to bottom or from bottom to top. But they can be irreversible, as when we perceive a ship first higher up and then lower down the stream. The perception of the ship higher up can only precede, and not follow, the perception of it lower down. 'Cause' is a rule applied to irreversible sequences in time.[13] The rule is that 'the condition under which an event invariably and necessarily follows is to be found in what precedes the event'.[14] 'Invariably' and 'necessarily' are elements in what Kant postulates to be the category of Cause. They are not my present concern; they would take us into questions beyond that of how Kant takes Cause as a category for ordering objective successions of perceptions in time, and I do not think that in the Second Analogy he does take us beyond this, even if some commentators try to say so.[15] Kant's view in the Second Analogy is that where perceptions occur in a series, and where some parts of the series can only be obtained after other parts, we speak of them as causally connected. Yet if we want to say not only that we have to perceive the boat lower down the stream after perceiving it higher up the stream, but also that its occupation of successive positions is caused, for example by its being propelled, then 'cause' will have to mean something stronger than the rule for ordering perceptions as succeeding each other irreversibly in time.

Schopenhauer saw this in his criticism of Kant's Second Analogy in *The Fourfold Root of the Principle of Sufficient Reason*. He does it by making (physical) causation one form of the general principle that we seek to understand a thing by connecting it with something else. Physical causation is a way of explaining changes of state in one thing by reference to changes in another, and this is not only an irreversible succession. Indeed, he says, 'Kant and Hume fell into opposite errors. Thus Hume declared all consequence to be mere sequence; Kant, on the other hand, affirmed that there is no other sequence but consequence.' Schopenhauer is here, of course, referring to sequences that we cannot order as we please; he makes the jibe against Hume that no one has been misled through custom and habit into regarding the succession of day and night as one being the cause of the other.[16]

On a more sophisticated view, a causal explanation of day succeeding night (and then night day) can of course be given by an account of the relation of the earth to the sun, and the rotation of the earth, placing this not just in a sequence but in a system. It might then fall under what Schopenhauer called 'physical causation'. He was, however, justified in asking whether Kant in fact gives us more than irreversible sequence in time. This links causation with the before and after relation in time.[17] This can go with the view of causation as a relation between events, since whatever else may be true of events, some of them precede others in time.

D. H. Mellor in *Real Time* also connects causation with the direction of time. Mellor however makes causation primary, deriving the direction of time from the irreversible relation between cause and effect. This links sequences of actual events, not just our perceptions of events in a before and after relation. Indeed, perceiving is itself an event normally following the event perceived, and this is given by Mellor as an instance of an event to be causally explained. Effects come after their causes. It is therefore essential for Mellor to deny the possibility of backward causation, where causes come after effects, and of causal loops of a kind where an effect does not have a feedback on a succeeding state in a series, but comes back on the original cause. Mellor deals, I find convincingly, with accounts of supposed backward causation, showing them to be inconsistent.[18] Science fiction-like accounts turn out as fantasies of how some local events might be reversed, but they presuppose an environment in which other events, including perceptions, go on in forward causation. So we have a one-way causal direction, in which the future may be predicted but not perceived, and the past may have been perceived but is not predicted, and in which our actions are expected to have effects in the future and not on the past.[19] 'Past', 'present' and 'future' are then defined through these 'before and after' characteristics of causation.

If the relation of before and after in the direction of time is to be derived from before and after in the sequence of cause and effect, then the causal order cannot just be a succession in time, unless the direction of time and the direction of causation are synonymous. Mellor wants a stronger view of causation than this, since he derives the direction of time from the direction of causation. Causation makes more likely that something having certain properties at one stage will have the same or certain other properties at another stage. Counterfactually, it licenses saying certain properties would have been different had certain other properties been different. But is this strong enough? We seem to be back to Russell's causal lines: causation as the possibility of predicting changes in properties.

The key term here is 'properties', and events which are changes are differences of properties at different times. (Not all events are changes; for instance the beginning of something is not a change). But the events themselves are still unchanging units. An event has temporal parts which can have different properties. But the event which has these temporal parts just is the event that has these parts; it does not change. The temporal parts are also events which do not change. There is no transition or movement from one part into the other, or from one event to another. So we still have a Zeno universe with 'before and after', but no changings. Mellor may not be unhappy with a Zeno universe. If, however, we are unhappy with a Zeno universe, and do not believe (as I do not) that we really live in one, it may be that our troubles are over causation as a relation either between events, or between properties of events at different times, as not allowing for movement and transition.

How difficult it is to avoid ending in a Zeno universe comes out even in Newton's dynamics. Newton's heart is in a world of forces and flows, where actions and reactions occur between moving bodies. In describing his 'Method of Fluxions', he writes about how he sees mathematical elements as generated from the continuous motions of points:

> Mathematical quantities I here consider not as consisting of indivisibles, either parts least possible or infinitely small ones, but as described by a continuous motion. Lines are described and by describing generated not through the apposition of parts but through the continuous motion of points; surface-areas are through the motion of lines, solids through the motion of surface-areas, angles through the rotation of sides, times through continuous flux, and the like in other cases. These geneses take place in the physical world and are daily enacted in the motion of bodies visibly before our eyes. And in much this manner the ancients, by 'drawing' mobile straight lines into stationary lines, taught the genesis of rectangles.
>
> By considering, then, that quantities increasing and begotten by increase in equal times come to be greater or lesser in accord with the greater or less speed with which they grow and are generated, I was brought to seek a method of determining quantities out of the speeds of motion or increment by which they are generated, and, naming these speeds of motion or increment 'fluxions' of the quantities generated, and the quantities so born 'fluents', I fell in the year 1665 upon the method of fluxions which I have formerly imparted to friends and which I have here employed in the quadrature of curves.[20]

So he started from 'flow' and derived change over an interval from the 'flow'. But the mathematics went the other way, and derived velocity from the change in an interval, presenting velocity at an instant, and motion as the occupation of a succession of states.

In Newton's account of forces actual motion also seems to get lost. His use of words like 'attraction', 'impulsion', 'resistance' suggests that he sees bodies as acting on each other with real propensities to produce changes in their motions. Yet his concern to avoid hypothesising occult causes producing these effects leads him at times to insist that he is using these terms only in a 'mathematical' and not in a physical sense.[21] He writes in *Definitio* VIII of the *Principia*:

> I . . . use the words attraction, impulse, or propensity of any sort towards a centre, promiscuously and indifferently, one for another; considering these forces not physically, but mathematically: wherefore the reader is not to imagine that by those words I anywhere take upon me to define the kind, or the manner of any action, the causes or

the physical reason thereof, or that I attribute forces in a true or physical sense, to certain centres (which are only mathematical points): when at any time I happen to speak of centres as attracting or as endued with attractive powers.[22]

He is concerned not with what forces are in themselves, but with how they are formulated in mathematical laws. 'Motion' is indeed basic (there are the Laws of Motion), but it is no longer, as in Aristotelian Physics, a property of bodies; it is a state, just as rest is a state, in which bodies persist uniformally, unless the state is changed by an external force as impression at an instant (except in gravity where he thought the force was instantaneous but acted over an extended interval). The physical notions of impression and impulsion producing changes of state are here present, but the emphasis is on the mathematical laws. Mathematically the force is reduced to an impulse at an instant, and velocity is measured at an instant. The notion of velocity at an instant strips the mathematics off from motion and change, for how can actual motion and change happen at an instant? Given the Laws of Motion and the position and velocity of a particle at an instant, what the mathematics does is to enable its position and velocity at another instant to be calculated, as also changes in position and velocity due to impact. Force is measured by the rate of change of momentum; so what we are presented with is a formula for the rate of change. Yet at the same time there is a presupposed background of bodies really moving, imparting movements to each other through their impacts, where 'action and reaction' are equal and opposite; and the magnificent picture of the world of Newtonian dynamics is drawn like this.

The reluctance to admit hidden causes may have been due to a fear of seeing forces as occult powers, rather than to a fear of seeing the forces as efficacious in changes, or as potentially efficacious, (as in a coiled spring). The fear could thus lead to substituting a mathematical formula for a description of how, not occultly but experientially, we find things do in fact move and change each other's movements by their impacts. The glory of Newtonian dynamics lay in combining this brute experience with a mathematical system of Laws of Motion. Motion, persistence in motion as inertia, and changes in motion, whether of rate of acceleration or of direction, are in fact thought of as occurring in nature. So motion, with communication of motion, is central to how one body causes a change of state in another.

In the Newtonian scheme, there were physical properties, such as gravity, not reducible to motion, though they influence it, and in later physics there are still others – such as electric charge, 'charm', 'strangeness'. Where changes are changes in motion, I have suggested that in the Newtonian account of forces as effecting changes of state, the actual movingness of moving bodies seems to get lost. I have already claimed that change is not sufficiently defined as difference of properties at different times. We need to get in the *changing* of one property into another, which is not just a succession of properties or a succession of states. Motion is involved in changes of place, and many changes of properties involve changes of place, or spatial redistributions. (There are of course changes such as those of brightness or temperature which may not involve changes of place, though they may involve spatial redistributions of constituent particles).

The Zeno universe had successive states or positions; it did not have transport from one to another. If we want to get out of a Zeno universe, we should, I think, start with motion as more than occupation of different places at different times; if we want to introduce causation into it, we shall need more than motion, but we can start there.

I began this chapter with events as candidates for being the particulars between which causal relations held, and said that this could lead to a view of units in succession, where transition was lost. Succession of events without transition may allow change to be a difference of properties at different times; it does not allow for their *changing*. Causation can be sequence, but can it be *consequence* if causal chains of events are described as though they were successions of 'stills'? A number of problems are piling up, and more are likely to come over what is called in the jargon the 'ontological status' of events; these problems may extend not only to whether events are the particulars between which causal relations hold, but to whether they are basic particulars at all.

3 Events and Non-events

The 1920s saw philosophers (for instance, Russell, Whitehead, Broad) recommend that events be seen not only as constituents in the world but as the only constituents. They wanted to get away from the metaphysics which had come down from Aristotle, where the primary constituents were substances sustaining attributes. Their event ontologies were worked out in the context of Relativity Theory, where 'events' were four-dimensional units, possibly of Space–Time. Things and even persons were to be seen as characters of events or series of events: Socrates was a long Socratic event, or a Socratic stretch of Space–Time. So in this ontology, events are not one kind of particular in a world which also contains other kinds of particulars. Everything is an event.

If events are space–time regions, even if Space–Time is thought of as a kind of stuff, as in General Relativity, it must have some properties other than spatio–temporal ones to give different regions enough stuffing to be distinguishable. Indeed, it might be thought that regions are distinguishable through events rather than events through regions. Quine, who wants to have an event ontology, in that he says physical objects considered four-dimensionally are not to be distinguished from events, marks out an event as 'the content, however heterogeneous, of some portion of space–time, however disconnected or gerrymandered'.[1] Such presumably, might be everything going on in this room from 11 a.m. to 11.10 a.m., and it would certainly take some gerrymandering to show this as one event. It has indeed 'content', but what unites it is spatio–temporal location.

Then does each space–time region define a single event? In a discussion with E. J. Lemmon,[2] Davidson says a number of events can occupy the same space–time zone. Jones can be swimming the Hellespont, catching a cold, and counting his blessings. How many events are there? Quine grasps the nettle (I do not know whether in reply to Davidson or in its own right) by saying that events that happen to take up the same portion of Space–Time would be one event. 'If a man whistled a song all the while he was walking to the bus stop and not a

17

moment more, then presumably the event of his whistling the song and the event of his walking to the bus would both be identified with the same temporal segment of the man.'[3]

Of course, to identify events with the contents of space–time zones is to give a technical and not (as Davidson does) an ordinary language definition. E. J. Lemmon, in the discussion with Davidson[4] says that it is necessary for the identity of events that they occupy the same space–time zone (which is surely right). However, I am not clear whether he only means that it is necessary that events are identified *by* occupation of a space–time zone, or that they are identical *with* it. He says 'We may even invoke a version of the identity of indiscernibles and identify events with *space–time zones*. Thus Jones buttering the toast *is* a space–time zone whose boundaries are included in what we may call the bathroom-slice determined by the period (say) 11.55 p.m.–12.05 a.m.'[5] Certainly these space–time zones must have contents, or properties, if they are to be distinguished and Lemmon speaks of persons and objects as participants in the zone event, while the event is identified by a space–time zone. But to be identified *by* is not the same as to be identical *with*.

So I come back to the need for events to have properties not derivable just from spatio–temporal location. In the end I shall want to say that something is going on in them, but that is another story. Moreover, if, with Quine, an event is identified with all the contents of a space–time zone, most events would need to be pretty gerrymandered. (I say, 'most' and not 'all', since there might be space–time zones in outer space in which the only content was one electron coming into existence. I do not know if this is empirically possible, but it would be logically possible).

Whitehead has a distinction which, I think, may be relevant to the Quinian view: that between an event and a duration.[6] A duration is the present state of the universe with all the concrete happenings in it from a standpoint (which may, but need not be, a conscious percipient). An event is the notion of a bounded slice of some going-on in a particular spatio–temporal spread, and it can be bounded as a long event extending over shorter events. So on the one hand we can have events, which are bounded and describable, but abstracted from their background. On the other hand we have durations which are unbounded and concrete, but only describable by being edited into events. The remedy may be to remember that 'events' are selected out of durations: they are not clear-cut entities which are also concrete particulars in their own right. Quine's 'events' seem to me to conflate these two notions. He wants to present events as concretely as he can; but by making an event *all* the contents of some portion of Space–Time, he turns it into something which we cannot possibly describe and talk about in a serviceable way. We can talk in a serviceable way about limited events, where each is only part of what may be going on in some portion of Space–Time. In the thorough-going event ontologies, such as Whitehead's and Russell's, where events were four-dimensional units, 'event' was a term of art; and what seems to have happened is that something of this has been carried over into a more 'ordinary language' view of an event, such as Davidson's. Quine is nearer to the older view, but his remarks about his event ontology are somewhat scanty.

Davidson claims that events exist as particulars because they can be quantified over in definite descriptions. Where two events are connected causally, this can be put in the form of a two-place predicate: the event of Brutus causing the death of Caesar by stabbing (allowing for the sake of the example that he did cause it, and did not only administer the unkindest cut of all) can be put:

$$\exists x \text{ (killing of Caesar } x).\exists y \text{ (stabbing by Brutus } y).\, y \text{ caused } x$$

Note that these descriptions of events take the form of 'verb nominalisations' – 'the killing of Caesar', not the fact-like form 'that Caesar was killed'. A statement of fact is a proposition, and there are problems about the relation of propositions to states of affairs. ('States of affairs' I take to be complexes of events; I think, but would not press, that they are called 'states of affairs' when the emphasis is on some special character: 'This is a dangerous situation'; 'Here's a pretty mess'.) Verb nominalisations get nearer than statements of fact to naming singular events. Also the causal connection between them (Caesar dying 'because' of being stabbed by Brutus) is less likely to confound 'because' with a truth-functional connection between propositions.

So, I declare myself on Davidson's side in going for gerundive nominalisations rather than fact-like statements for describing events. But are we sure that there is nothing fishy about events? I have spoken of an event as a happening which can be noted and described. So if 'facts' are proposition-like, events are description-like. How do we get behind the description? One way could be by having a criterion for when two descriptions refer to the same event. There is a term in the literature, 'transparency'; transparency, however, is not all that transparent, as it might be if it meant that we can see the event through the description. 'Transparency' means that a descriptive phrase can be substituted for another with the same reference and it will have the same truth values. So 'The Titanic struck an iceberg' refers to the same event as 'The largest liner afloat in 1912 struck an iceberg'. If the former statement is true, so also is the latter.

This gives co-reference to the same event, where two descriptions are genuinely substitutable without changing their truth values. The meaning is said to be extensional, that is given by reference, and not affected by an attitude of mind on the part of whoever states them. Two events can also be said to be the same if they have the same causal relations. But this can conflict with the extensional criterion of one description being substitutable for another. A causal statement may be true of an event under one description which would not be true of it under another. A causal factor can come in because the meaning is intensional, depending on a state of mind in the person who understood it. Two intensional statements may have the same reference, but one may be true as a causal statement and the other is not. Oedipus killed Laius; he killed an angry old man at a crossroads; and this event was also (unbeknown to him) his killing his father. But Oedipus subsequently experienced guilt because he had killed his father and then married his mother. His state could also be described as being married to Jocasta; but if he had not come to know that she was his mother and Laius was his father, he would not have experienced guilt.[7] So here is an effect of the marriage under one description which would not be given as an effect under the other. The effect depended on an intensional feature present in one description but not present in the other. 'Having married his mother' meant something very different to Oedipus from 'having married Jocasta', and the effects of the event in producing guilt are explained through the former description and not through the latter.

Nevertheless, the suggestion that we try to get at the particular event behind the descriptions through thinking about causal relations does, I think, give us a clue. But it is a clue which will lead us into the problems over event causation and this is a later story. (If we conclude that it is not events themselves which are causes, we shall not have the circularity of Davidson's view, where events are causes and are also identified by their causal relations.)

When we speak of a singular event as caused or as having effects, this is said to be explanatory when it can be connected with some generalisation – this need not be as elevated as a Law; it can be a commonsensical generalisation as that ships which get great gashes in their holds so that water pours in are likely to sink (the law would be that of the specific gravity of water). So the singular event has a property or properties by which it can be assigned to a class of events, and it is followed by another event whose property or properties also assign it to a class, and a causal generalisation can be made by stating a relation between properties of events of these two classes. The causal statement about a particular event is being made about it as an instance of a kind, and under the description which assigns it to the kind named by these properties. This turns attention from events to their properties, or to the properties of the objects which are said to enter into them.

Jaegwon Kim[8] has a view of events as exemplifications of properties which are constitutive properties of objects. An event is a concrete object or a *n*-tuple of objects exemplifying a property at a time. In the event of my falling downstairs, I may not feel very like a concrete object, but one sees what he means; it is less easy to say what property is exemplified in my falling downstairs: perhaps 'batteredness'. An event can have many properties; so can objects. A constitutive property is, I think, the property without which the object could not enter into that event. So in 'Socrates drinking hemlock', the constitutive property of Socrates is being a drinker of hemlock, not for example being snub-nosed. 'Being a drinker of hemlock' becomes a constitutive property of a particular event by being exemplified at a particular time. I have said 'a particular event' because properties can also be constitutive of what Kim calls 'generic events', for example *a* drinking of hemlock; causation is seen as a regular conjunction of the constitutive properties of two generic events: a drinking of hemlock is regularly connected with a dying. Thus causation is seen by Kim as a Hume-like regular conjunction between the properties of generic events, and this is the role of the general conjunctions which may or may not be dignified by the name of laws. They hold between generic events whose properties when exemplified at particular times constitute particular events.

If the constitutive property of an event is the constitutive property of its object or objects at a time, this gets objects into the event through their properties. But what seems to have got lost is the event as something *happening* to something, and not just exemplifying its constitutive property at a time.[9] I think to describe events like 'drinking hemlock', as 'verb nominalisations' gets nearer to this than calling them exemplifications of a property, even with the crucial addition 'at a time', since a verb nominalisation at least can be held to name an event as an occurrence.

To call events 'occurrences' might seem just to be producing a synonym; but 'event' has become something of a term of art in the literature, whereas I do not think this fate has yet befallen 'occurrence'. Moreover, an occurrence has the tone of something actually occurring, whereas 'event' has acquired the tone of an outcome, an *eventum*. The *eveniens*, which is something happening in time, has got lost. The events are particulars which as bounded units do not change. This obviously applies to descriptions of events: an event under that description just is that event under that description. It cannot change in the middle of it. If I speak of the event of my falling downstairs, there may have been changes in me as I fell from the first stair to the second, and so on till I fell from the eleventh stair to the floor at the bottom. But though these may be temporal parts or stages in my falling downstairs, they are not changes in the event described as 'my falling downstairs'. I can however divide the event of falling downstairs into shorter events: falling from the first to the second stair, and so on, till we come to my falling from the eleventh stair to the ground. Whitehead, who had an event ontology, at any rate in his earlier books, spoke of a longer event (for example the falling downstairs) as 'extending over' shorter events (the falling from one stair to the next).[10] Since there are various ways in which we could cut up a long event into segments over which it could extend, this is a way in which the number of events can be multiplied without any presumed change in what is actually going on. Whitehead does indeed have a 'passage of nature' which is a changing process. But his events themselves do not change, though they can extend over others and be extended over by others. So change could be a way of saying that shorter events can be presented as segments of a longer event. It would look, then, as though any longer event can be segmented into shorter events at any point, so that there could be an indefinite number of events. How can real particulars be created *ad lib* by merely geometrical subdivision?

D. H. Mellor has a view of events as having temporal parts which could avoid this difficulty.[11] An event has temporal parts which are also events, but these parts cannot be formed by segmenting it any old how. Each has to be a causal unit, otherwise it would not be an event. So each sub-event which is a temporal part of a longer event will have its own causal properties or property which may be investigated as a mechanism (*modus operandi?*) contributing to the longer event; these causal properties cannot be shown by making arbitrary cuts in the longer event. Whitehead may have been coming to something like this, put in very different language, in his later books, where a 'long event' is called a 'route of actual occasions', and each actual occasion is a unit with causal properties. Whitehead's 'actual occasions' are the smallest units which function causally; so they cannot be sub-divided into further temporal parts. They are also called 'actual entities', and I think that as basic units they differ more than he recognises from the events of his earlier ontology.

If events have temporal parts, what should one say about the beginning and the end of some process? These surely are events, and, it would seem, have no temporal parts. Here one must bear in mind the distinction between the description of an event and its actual occurrence. Its description as a beginning or an ending does not have temporal parts; nor indeed does any description have temporal parts. The beginning or ending as actually occurring cannot, I think, be a point-instant with no spatio–temporal extension. An event as *eveniens*, happening, cannot be even instantaneous, if this means having no duration. The beginning of a process as occurring would be its initial stage from, so to say, the word go; the ending would be the terminal stage up to the finishing point. What may be the shortest time in which anything has occurred is an empirical matter on which there may be no accepted answer. A letter headed 'Momentous Incidents' in *The Times* of 4 December 1982 from Professor Sir George Porter of the Davy Faraday Laboratory runs:

> Sir, Your correspondent in New York (December 2) who reports 'The briefest event ever recorded' has not kept up with the times. Picosecond (thousandth of a billionth of a second) events have been measured almost routinely for several years and the record at present is 30 times shorter still – or 30 femtoseconds.

I return to the claim of events to be causal units. In the event ontologies of the early Whitehead and Russell, everything was an event; events were not one kind of particular in a world which also contained other kinds, such as things and persons. Even so, events have to be described through properties, and if they are causal units this is likely to be put in terms of properties. There are also objects with properties. For Mellor, changes in properties of objects[12] are events, though not all events are changes; something coming into existence is not a change, except in what Mellor says is a contrived sense, such as a change in the universe. Causation allows the likelihood of prediction of properties at a later time from those at an earlier time. Prediction suggests the hypothetical dispositional view of property; it is something which would be observed if . . . . Mellor, however, is saying more than this; the prediction of the properties at a later stage is licensed by the properties at an earlier stage being what they are. That is, the properties are not just dispositional as hypotheticals, in the sense that if certain circumstances occurred, certain happenings would be observed, so that '*a* is fragile' means that if *a* were dropped, it would break. In an earlier paper, Mellor defended a view of dispositions as having a categorical basis; they are not just subjunctives (what would happen if . . .).[13] Dispositions are usually ascribed when their displays are regarded as possible. But if precautions are taken to make a display impossible, for example by making impossible the conditions in which a fuel would explode, this would not mean that the fuel was not explosive. 'It is ridiculous to say that their success robs the fuel of its explosive disposition and thus the precautions of their point.' So causal explanation through dispositional properties calls for real properties which can have effects. The explanation of these will need evidence independent of the mere dispositional property; that glass is fragile is caused by other properties of the glass, namely by its molecular composition, and this does not entail that it breaks when dropped. Fragility is thus a real categorical property, not translatable into a subjunctive saying what would happen were it dropped. There is indeed a chance that a fragile glass might not break when dropped. The glass broke because it was dropped: yes, but its being fragile made dropping it a cause of its breaking, and it was fragile because of its molecular composition. The dropping is an event, but it is causal because of properties, of which the change is the effect. So the presence of real properties in something is not only a necessary condition for the display of its other properties, but the real properties are in some way generative of other properties at a later stage. I do not know whether Mellor would accept the word 'generative', in spite of his stressing the word 'effects'.

A philosopher who would accept this word is Sidney Shoemaker. He holds that a thing's real properties are shown through their contribution to its 'causal powers' in producing effects (including, it would seem, in our perceptions).[14] This produces a circularity, if identity of a property is identity of causal powers, and causal powers are taken to define 'identity'. Shoemaker defends the circularity, in saying that philosophy is concerned with internal relations between concepts. In fact 'causal powers' do not define the identity of a property; rather, they are means of distinguishing between what Shoemaker calls a 'real property' and a 'mere Cambridge property'.[15] This comes out in his invoking causation as a relation between a thing's properties at one stage and its properties at a later stage.

What properties are instantiated in later stages of a genuine history i.e. of a persisting thing is a function of, among other things, what properties were instantiated at earlier stages of it. In the simplest case, where the thing has minimal interaction with other things and has minimal internal complexity, the causal connections linking the stages will be what I shall call 'property preserving' ones, and will result in similarity between successive stages. Such similarity is often used as evidence of identity, but as I have just argued, it is evidence of identity only as far as it is evidence of counterfactual dependence which in turn I take to indicate a causal relationship.[16]

So here properties of things, not events, are the units of causal relations, and properties are signs of causal powers if counterfactual statements can be made about them.

The counterfactual would be that if A had not had certain properties at stage S it would not have had certain properties at stage S_1. This dependence of a later property on an earlier one does not apply to all properties, but only to those whose acquisition or loss constitutes a genuine change in the thing. There can be 'mere Cambridge changes'. These follow the criterion that 'The thing called X has changed if we have "$F(X)$ at time t" true and "$F(X)$ at time t_1" false for some interpretation of "F", "t" and "t_1" '. All changes satisfy this criterion, but some which satisfy it are not 'real changes' and these are 'mere Cambridge changes'; thus Socrates would undergo a change when he came to be shorter than Theaetetus because of the latter's growth. It could nevertheless be said that Theaetetus' growth caused Socrates to have a relational property he did not have before, *viz*, that of being shorter than Theaetetus. But this does not give Socrates a property which would be likely to appear in an account of his properties as causal powers, which is what Shoemaker is interested in. He therefore speaks of 'mere Cambridge properties', as well as 'mere Cambridge changes'. It is said that 'being shorter than Theaetetus' does not produce a change in Socrates. Might it not do so supposing *per impossible* it made him feel jealous? One cannot say out of context what would be a 'mere Cambridge change'.

Shoemaker is concerned to see not only change but also identity as more than a matter of difference or resemblance between successive states: so much so that he makes both of these depend on the manifestations of causal potentialities in a thing's 'real properties' (as distinct from its 'mere Cambridge properties'). 'The essence of a property . . . consists in its potential for contributing to the causal powers of the things that have it. A power, in turn, is specified by saying what will happen if the thing that has it is placed in various circumstances, or interacts in certain ways with other things.'[17] As with Mellor's 'dispositions', a property's potentiality for what would happen in certain circumstances is grounded in what it already is when not being displayed, though of course what it is may be discovered through its power to effect other things. Shoemaker uses strong language about these properties as 'powers'; and I take him to mean honest to goodness powers to produce effects, not just potentials as hypothetical propositions which would become categorical if certain circumstances obtained. That would take us back to the merely subjunctive view of dispositions – what would happen if – which both he and Mellor reject. For Mellor, however, the properties which come into causal explanations are those whose identities are given in the theories in which they appear. So for Newton inertial mass is one property, though it accounts for many dispositions under different forces. It is the linking of dispositional properties with laws and projectibility in prediction which distinguishes them from 'mere Cambridge properties'.[18]

What is gained is that cause is connected with real properties of things. Thus both Shoemaker and Mellor escape troubles over event causation, since they do not see events as causes, but as needing to be causally explained. Scientifically causation has explanatory power if the real properties are instances of general laws; this brings in more than Shoemaker's speaking of them as having "causal powers". There is something right, therefore, in Kim's seeing a causal *explanation* as linking properties of generic events. But the actual event which is an instance of the generalisation in the explanation is singular and not generic, and its properties, even though generalisable, are due, when they are causal, to properties of its actual constituents. This is better taken care of by Mellor's view of dispositional properties of objects as propensities, and his holding that it is these that are causal, whereas the events in which they are displayed are caused.

Nevertheless, I have difficulty over Mellor's events. They occur at different times, and 'different times' are fixed in a before and after relation of dated events by reference to a token reflexive 'now'. My sitting here now at 9.30 a.m. is preceded by my having sat down at 9.15 and will probably be followed by my getting up at 11.30. The main concern of Mellor's book is to attack the notion of a tensed 'flow' of time, with past, present and future as more than this 'before' and 'after' dating. There may indeed be no 'flow' of time apart from processes which are measured temporarily. Where I differ from Mellor is that (I think) he not only dismisses a tensed flow of time, but also loses actual transitions and processes of becoming. We are given successions of events. They are in an irreversible order, and have temporal parts, each of which is dated as standing in a before or after relation to others. What I miss here is that an event should not only succeed another, but come into being, pass into another, and pass away, and this applies also to its temporal parts. No doubt as described, events are given as unchanging units. Taken as an ontology, this gave us a Zeno universe in which transition got lost. This came from fastening on the description of an event, not on its occurring. If we are thinking of its description, we can lose sight of it as something happening to something or somebody in a changing world. And in that case it could be a non-event.

So there are troubles over events as basic particulars, and troubles in store over event causation. Yet that is still a dominant model, and more needs to be said about it.

4 Event Causation

Most of those who speak of causation as event causation, including latter-day Humeans, accept that it must include more than observed regularities in sequences of events. Observed regularities might support generalisations based on induction by simple enumeration, but this gives a precarious basis for predictions as to future sequences. A causal account claims to be an explanation; though an explanation is not only a prediction, it looks to prediction for its confirmation. If a sequence shows a regularity in how things happen now, it should also obtain in how they will be found to happen. Hume saw that we need inductive generalisation from a number of cases; if there is predictive confidence the latter may be a matter of expectation based on custom – we have found A's to be followed by B's, so we have a customary expectation that they will continue to be so followed. But they may not. Russell called the reliance on habit 'animal induction',[1] and gave the example of the chicken whose master comes every morning to feed it, encouraging this agreeable expectation, until the day comes when he wrings its neck, thereby disappointing its simple faith in the order of nature. Yet we do have a simple faith ('*Aber Glaube*', as Waismann said) that there are orders of causal sequence which are not just resemblances; and we need more than repetition for causal explanation.[2] Moreover, we need to be able to deal with counterfactual suppositions: something X which did not happen might have happened if something else, Y had happened. We cannot observe sequences of things which did not happen, but we can speculate about them and this gives us play. So we need not only observed resemblances, but observed resemblances which license predictions that they will be sustained, or might have been sustained, and the license has to be more than the chicken's simple faith. It can be more than this if the generalisations about regular sequences are not simple inductive generalisations, but can be shown to follow from higher level general statements in a deductive theory, with a prediction that they will be found to obtain in future observations, or would have been found to obtain if some other condition had been present. In other words, the statements of regularities can be fitted into a hypothetico-deductive system.

This is R. B. Braithwaite's view in *Scientific Explanation*.[3] The higher level generalisations he calls 'nomic' universals (a term of W. E. Johnson's)[4], constituting natural laws, while the lower level observed similarities constitute 'universals of fact'. Neither of these kinds is necessary (the 'necessary' element is contained in the deduction within the system). They show 'contingent facts about the comprehensive character of various kinds of simple regularities and similarities', as Mary Hesse puts it in her essay 'A revised regularity view of scientific laws', in the *Festschrift* for R. B. Braithwaite.[5] Mary Hesse here follows on from Braithwaite's view in his *Scientific Explanation*. She goes further in showing how in the *development* of theories there is an internal self-correcting interplay between inductive judgements of perceived similarities and the use of theory in filtering out relevant from coincidental similarities. If generalisations (which can be probabilistic generalisations) can be put in the context of a wider theoretical system, this allows particular causal statements to be given stronger explanatory power as instances of laws. This can be called 'nomic subsumption'. An event *Y* is said to be caused by an event *X* if *Y*-like events are deducible from *X*-like events with the aid of a known law. Or, more precisely, a singular case of a cause can be shown to be an instance of a conjunction of a certain kind deducible from a known law. What is the instance? The usual answer, we have said, is an event. What we are given in 'event causation' is a form of explanation relating statements which are descriptions of events to general statements about kinds of events. This form of explanation links statements describing events, and allows us to predict what events with similar descriptions will be likely to be observed in the future. Regularities in the observed events need to be formulated in a generalisation, which should be deducible from a higher order generalisation or law. No stronger connection between the events needs to be assumed.

If, however, it is said that *A* happened because *B* happened, what of the causal connective 'because'? It has been said that causal sentences referring to events in sequences are extensional. Extensionality is associated with truth functionality; that is to say, a proposition can be substituted for another with the same truth value, and a combination of propositions can be substituted for another combination with the same truth values. So if in 'The Titanic sank because she struck an iceberg' there is substituted 'Argentina won the World Cup in 1978' for 'The Titanic sank', the combination of this with 'she struck an iceberg' would have the same truth value, 'because' here being no more than the connective 'and' between the two sentences. This is not only wildly counter-intuitive; it could mean that anything might cause anything; also a 'cause' sentence and an 'effect' sentence could be reversed. So 'John kicked Paul and Paul fell down the stairs' could become 'Paul fell down the stairs and John kicked Paul'. But this ordering will not describe the same situation if Paul fell down the stairs *because* John kicked him. It is generally held that the time ordering is irreversible for the causal order, and the 'before' and 'after' relation is not a truth-functional one. So a more defensible view of the extensionality of causal sentences is that they can be 'co-referential'. Two causal sentences are co-referential if they refer to the same event.[6] So 'The Titanic sank' can refer to the same event as 'The largest liner in 1912 sank', and be followed by 'because she struck an iceberg.'

Such differences of description giving co-reference to the same event are not difficult to defend. What is difficult are changes of description which do not seem to have any plausible place in the causal context. So Miss Anscombe[7] says that if in 'There is an international crisis because "moi" de Gaulle made a speech', one substituted for ' "moi" de Gaulle' 'the man with the longest nose in France', this would not be plausible as a causal statement. This is because 'having the longest nose' is not an aspect causally relevant to the production of the crisis. Causal relevance brings in an explanatory interest, and this is an intensional and not an extensional matter.[8] The issue then becomes whether the aspect named is one which can be plausibly connected with a general characteristic which might be likely to have causal explanatory power. It might be plausible to substitute 'The President of France' for ' "moi" de Gaulle', since Presidents of France are a class of people who are in a position to cause international crises. Men with long noses are not such a class.[9]

The motive of the extensionalists in explaining events under certain descriptions is, however, to go behind interests, which are admitted to be intensional, and to refer to the particular events to which the descriptions apply. Davidson notably wrestles with this, since he wants causal explanations to refer to singular cases. The form of causal explanation he espouses is one where an event described by a singular term is an instance of a class which can be subsumed under a general rule. Yet, as he says,[10] 'there is an important difference between explaining the fact that there was *an* explosion in the broom cupboard and explaining the occurrence of *the* explosion in the broom cupboard. Explanation of the second sort touches the particular event as closely as language can ever touch any particular.' How closely does it touch it? 'The explosion in the broom cupboard' is the name of an event. There may have been a number of events occurring in the broom cupboard – a gas leak and a short circuit in the electric wiring (the installations for meters of both being lodged in the broom cupboard). The event could be further specified so as to bring in some of these other conditions. Would it then be the same event?

The criterion Davidson gives for different descriptions referring to the same event is sameness of causes and effects. The logical form of causal statements, he holds, should be presented in a two place predicate calculus, with an existential quantifier for a singular case. So 'The Titanic sank because she struck an iceberg' becomes 'Striking an iceberg caused the sinking of the Titanic'. This could be formalised as:

$(\exists x)$ (sinking x). (of the Titanic x). $(\exists y)$ (striking y). (an iceberg y). by the Titanic y). (y caused x)

The connective. (fullstop) for 'and' stands between phrases which are nominalisations referring to events.

Davidson works harder than most to maintain this reference to a particular singular event. But he says he abjures the analysis of the causal relation itself '.[11] What he does give is a view of its logic, along with a conviction that there is an ontology of events between which causal relations hold. This is supported by the view that where different descriptions nominate events which have the same causes and effects, they are the same event. There is a peculiarly foolish young woman, Flora, whose misfortune in getting a skin rash from drying herself with a coarse towel is now well ensconsed in the literature (Davidson started this example off).[12] Flora's drying her sensitive skin with a coarse towel caused a skin rash; if Flora did this, then her drying herself with a towel caused a skin rash, and this less full description refers to the same event, since the cause and effect are the same. The former version specifies further the aspects of the event which can be connected with a causal law – presumably one stating the damaging effects of the friction of abrasive material on delicate organic tissues. Here the sameness of reference does not seem to constitute a problem. But there is a problem if sameness of events is defined by sameness of causal relation, and if a description of an event is modified by an adverb which may indicate an additional causal factor. Beauchamp and Rosenberg,[13] using the well-worn example, claim that if one said 'The Titanic striking an iceberg caused the sinking of the Titanic', and then said 'The Titanic striking an iceberg caused the Titanic's rapid sinking', one might be referring to a different event, in that the *rapidity* of the sinking might have been due to faulty orders concerning the closing of hatches (or whatever one can close on such occasions). In that case, the causal relations in the two statements would not be the same, and so they would not refer to the same event. Beauchamp and Rosenberg, in their concern to keep up the view that causal statements are extensional, are prepared to draw the heroic conclusion that the Titanic's sinking by striking an iceberg and the Titanic sinking rapidly are different events, because what is causally true of the one need not be causally true of the other. So an adverb modifying a description of an event can make it name a different event: 'the event's being rapid or fatal or unexpected is itself an event, or at least an entity quite distinct from the event modified. This line of argument of course results in a multiplication of events . . . '[14] Yes, indeed; as many as there can be modifying adverbs, if the modification adds another causal factor to the description. I do not think Davidson would accept this, since on his view of the logic of causal statements, where further specifications of the event are added as what he calls 'adverbial modifiers'[15], the earlier clauses in the formula are entailed by the later ones. Thus is the example of the Titanic sinking rapidly, which can be formalised:

$$\exists x \ (\text{sinking } x) . (\text{of the Titanic } x) . (\text{rapidly } x)$$

'the Titanic sinking rapidly' entails 'the Titanic sinking', and so 'rapidly' can be detached.

However, there is a difficulty over saying that an adverb can be detached on the score that the expression extended by the adverb entails the unextended expression. Sometimes the adverb or adverbial phrase modifies the sense of the whole expression. So in '*A* was often drunk on New Year's Eve' does not entail '*A* was often drunk'.[16] That is to say, some adverbs are genuinely modifiers of the meaning of the expression, and if these are detached, the statement without them may not be true.

However, Davidson's view that detaching adverbial modifiers by entailment allows a truncated description to refer to the same event as a fuller description is not a view of the meaning of the descriptions. It is a claim that the event under both descriptions has the same cause, on his criterion of identifying events through their causal relations. Davidson holds there can be total causes which may be only partly specified. In giving fuller descriptions of the event, further features are specified which may turn out to be relevant to the generalisation under which the total cause of the complex event may be subsumed. This does not mean that more truncated descriptions may not refer to the same event, but further necessary conditions may need to be included to find the cause which is an instance of a general law: Davidson[17] cites Brutus' stabbing of Caesar.

We may suppose there is some predicate '$P(x, y, e)$' true of Brutus, Caesar, and Brutus' stabbing of Caesar and such that any stab (by anyone) that is P is followed by the death of the stabbed. And let us suppose further that this law meets Mill's requirements of being *unconditional* – it supports counterfactuals of the form 'If Cleopatra had received a stab that was P, she would have died.' Now we can prove (assuming a man dies only once) that Brutus' stab was sufficient for Caesar's death. Yet it was not the cause of Caesar's death, for Caesar's death was the death of a man with more wounds than Brutus inflicted, and such a death could not have been caused by an event that was P ('P' was chosen to apply only to stabbings administered by a single hand). The trouble here is not that the description of the cause is partial, but that the event described was literally (spatio–temporally) only part of the cause.

I think there is a difficulty here over giving a necessary condition as part of a total sufficient cause. An aspect of this difficulty has been brought out by Gerald Vision in a note on 'Causal Sufficiency'.[18] He says Davidson's account does not distinguish between specifying the partial cause and specifying only a part of the whole cause. As a palmary instance of what might be called a partial cause he gives the last straw that breaks the camel's back. But this might be turned into a whole cause as being an instance of a generalisation such as: 'the placing of a straw on the back of a camel which already has n litres on its back, such and such a spinal structure, etc.' This would resemble the Brutus' stab example, if we were to suppose Brutus' stab was a 'last straw' in giving a final *coup de grâce*.

In this case, the partial cause is the last effective member of a series of events. Then it would be a factor selected by spatio–temporal proximity. Yet in some cases other factors not in immediate temporal proximity may be selected as causes.[19] In all these cases, some reason is given for the selection, and other conditions without which this factor would not be sufficient are recognised or assumed as necessary. To make this factor not a partial cause (which indeed may be the relevant one in the context in which it is cited), but part of the total cause, the other necessary conditions would have to be built into the description of the 'total cause'. (I shall be querying the notion of a 'total cause'.)

L. J. O'Neill defends Davidson's view of partial and total causes in a note 'Singular Causal Statements'.[20] A partial description of an event – we again meet the unfortunate Flora drying herself with a towel – can become a partial description of a total cause of another event, Flora getting a skin rash, if it is extended (co-extensionally) into a total description – 'Flora drying herself by rubbing her sensitive skin with a coarse towel'. Here the fuller description would be more likely to show a causal connection with an eruption of a skin rash than would 'Flora drying herself with a towel', though it describes the same event. It pinpoints the features which can be connected with an *appropriate* law (in this case it would be one about the probable effects of friction on delicate organic tissue).

So in the Titanic example the appropriate law would be Archimedes' law of specific gravity, where if a hollow container and its contents are lighter than the volume of water it displaces it will float, and if not, it will sink. There is not a law that ships which strike icebergs sink; they sink if they are holed and enough water gets in. In the story as filled out by Beauchamp and Rosenberg, it is suggested (very likely falsely, but that does not affect the argument) that an additional factor causing the *rapid* sinking could have been the negligence of the captain in failing to give orders to shut down hatches.

The event which is connected with the appropriate law (here Archimedes' law) might not have happened, or happened as rapidly as it did, without the presence of other conditions. But if we have to build all these into the law giving the total cause, we shall get some very bizarre laws. I am pretty sure that Davidson wants covering laws to be like Archimedes', not generalisations including all the conditions sufficient for the effect. In that case, he would not have to say with Beauchamp and Rosenberg that any addition to the description which introduces another contributory condition turns it into a description of another event. He would surely say that the Titanic sinking is the same event as the Titanic sinking rapidly. The selection of a feature which can be connected with an appropriate law is not the same as the citing of all the conditions necessary and sufficient for the event to happen in the way it did in the singular instance – if this is indeed what is meant by a total cause. The trouble is in the expression 'total cause'. Causal explanations have to select among the conditions; and I agree with Vision, when he comes back at O'Neill,[21] in saying that O'Neill is giving Davidson's view of causal explanation, not of singular causal statements. These cite conditions selected from a context, and may properly give only part of a cause or a partial description of a total cause. I should claim that causal explanations, given through descriptions of events, *can* only give partial causes, in that the statements citing them hold in the singular case only if certain background conditions are taken for granted. Nevertheless on the Davidsonian model we shall look for (though he admits we may not be able to find) a background law of which the feature selected as explanatory is an instance. If another feature is selected because of a different explanatory interest in a different context, then, I suggest, another law, or a generalisation about the kind of thing that might be expected, may be appealed to. A court of inquiry might attribute the sinking of the Titanic to the captain's negligence in maintaining a racing speed in dangerous waters; and the iceberg would then produce the condition through which the captain's negligence caused a disaster.[22] Different causal explanations can validly refer to the same complex event if the covering laws and generalisations behind them are such as not to be conflicting, but supplement each other in explaining more features of the event. But this does not mean that as explanatory they can coalesce into a single total cause. In causal explanation, if we look for a feature of a kind deducible from a covering law, this will have to be picked out from the other background conditions, some of which may be necessary conditions in the particular case. Mill puts the problem when he says:[23]

It is seldom, if ever, between a consequent and a single antecedent that this invariable sequence subsists. It is usually between a consequent and the sum of several antecedents; the concurrence of all of them being requisite to produce, that is, to be certain of being followed by, the consequent. In such cases it is very common to single out one only of the antecedents under the denomination of Cause, calling the others merely Conditions. Thus, if a person eats of a particular dish, and dies in consequence, that is, would not have died if he had not eaten of it, people would be apt to say that eating of that dish was the cause of his death. There need not, however, be any invariable connection between eating of the dish and death; but there certainly is, among the circumstances which took place, some combination or other on which death is invariably consequent: as, for instance, the act of eating of the dish, combined with a particular bodily constitution, a particular state of present health, and perhaps even a certain state of the atmosphere; the whole of which circumstances perhaps constituted in this particular case the *conditions* of the phenomenon, or, in other words, the set of antecedents which determined it, and but for which it would not have happened. The real

Cause is the whole of these antecedents; and we have, philosophically speaking, no right to give the name of cause to one of them exclusively of the others.

Indeed, if it said that the total cause should include all the necessary conditions, and also be backed by a general law, then the law would seem to run into something of the same difficulty as we find over the Universalisability criterion of a rule for right actions in ethics when applied to difficult cases. If it would be right for A to commit a murder in such and such circumstances, it would be right for anyone else, say B, to commit a murder in similar circumstances. The more you specify the detailed circumstances, which in some stories might be pretty bizarre, then the less likely it is that there will be another case to which the very detailed rule would apply.

If all necessary conditions are included in a total cause which can be an instance of a general rule, Mill says that there will be some combination of circumstances on which the result 'invariably' follows. We could, no doubt, make this a matter of high probability, and waive 'invariably'. But even so, the greater the number of conditions included in the 'concurrence' needed to produce the effect, the more difficult it will be to produce a plausible law covering them all, and the more difficult to produce a number of sequences in which it is seen to be exemplified. The difficulty indeed lies in the notion of a 'total cause'. 'Cause' if it is to be used as an explanatory notion, will have to be used selectively, where other conditions not included in 'the cause' are being taken for granted. The nomic subsumption view is a pattern of causal explanation which looks for observable repeated sequences which can then be deduced from general laws. So it singles out causal lines as linear sequences which can be distinguished from other conditions in complex situations. Other conditions will be contributory factors in the complex situation; so, as Popper says, to give a causal explanation of an event can be to deduce a statement which describes it using as premises of the deduction one or more universal laws, together with certain singular statements, as initial conditions.[24] Thus, if a weight of 2 lb is put on a thread with a prehensile strength of 1 lb the prediction is that the thread will break. Here is the law-like statement. But that in this situation Jack was silly enough to use this thin piece of thread because he was in too much of a hurry to go and look for a thicker one could also be given as a causal explanation of the breaking. This is the 'select factor' form of causal explanation which can avoid the difficulties over 'partial' and 'total' causes.[25]

Actions can enter into this kind of causal explanation. Actions are described through intentions; in 'agency causation' this is the form in which they are explained. Davidson is well aware that we talk in terms of agency causation, and that for some practical purposes this will be taken as explanatory. But unlike explanation in event causation, no general law can be cited. As he says, 'no law lurks'.[26] Actions might get into event causation by being described in terms of beliefs and desires, as events, but he sees no general psycho–physiological laws behind these. Thus if we invoke agency causation, it is said not to fit into the model of event causation; it is assumed that we take model of event causation as the proper model of causal explanation. This is the assumption that can, indeed, I think must, be questioned.

Event causation looks to sequences of events as unchanging units; where these events are seen as causes and effects, this is in virtue of resemblances of properties in a number of sequences which can be generalised through a law. This model (a Humean one) is plausible as an epistemology of causal relations within a hypothetico–deductive view of scientific explanation. It fastens on properties given in descriptions of events, and causation is a principle licensing the prediction of similarities or differences of properties at different times. But 'events' here are edited descriptions of features of what is actually going on. When we ask what is actually going on, events are occurrences which come and go, and their descriptions record something happening to the participants in these occurrences. Event causation is a view contrived to fit these descriptions. The events so described record adventures of their participants. They are not basic particulars in their own right. True, they can be referred to in definite descriptions, and can be quantified over, and in this sense can be said to exist. But if their existence depends on their having participants whose adventures they record, and if causation is something which happens in the real world, it will come through the actions (in some sense of 'action') of these participants on each other. Those who claim events are basic particulars sometimes say that, for example, a flash of lightning can be an event without having participants. I do not see this. The flash happens because there are electrically charged particles about. When the lightning strikes a tree, the action comes from these, not just from the flash. If it is said that the appearance of a flash is an event, then there is a percipient in the situation to see it as a flash. The urge to exclude participants may come from an assumption that these should be material objects; they may be persons, or systems of very short duration. They certainly need not be unchanging substances, which were the main target for upholders of event ontologies. Some of the participants in events may be human agents acting on their environment and producing changes in it through their bodily movements, some may be non-human physical bodies. The word 'action' is sometimes considered only to be properly used of human actions. It is, however, normally extended in speaking, for example of the action and reaction of chemical substances on each other. If 'action' is thought to be too closely wedded to intentionality (though 'reaction' is not), we might perhaps speak of 'impact' and 'operation'. For there to be impacts and operations more is needed than a succession of events. There need to be transactions among the participants in the events, and these are lost in the account of event causation.

Events (or I prefer to say occurrences, event having become so much a term of art) happen in a world of movements and operations where change goes on in processes and does not only register that things have different properties at different times. I realise that to say the world is like this is controversial but, since it seems to me evident that it is, I want a view which gives causal explanations a substructure in terms of what Coleridge called 'goings-on', and not of what he called 'fixities and definites'. Otherwise we may be left with causation in a Zeno universe.

I see the substructure as one of operations between participants in events, and some of these operations are interventions of human agents. There is indeed a difficulty in seeing how to insert agency causation into a world where causation is described through event causation. There are difficulties in looking for mental events as causes; and if causes are physical events, we seem to lose agency. Yet we do not want to be left with just two different *façons de parler*, or even, in the end, just two different kinds of explanation. If we restrict causation to being a way of connecting ordered sequences as observed, and remove agency from this account, we could get something like the Kantian view of the phenomenal world as ordered under the category of empirical causation, and human action as autonomous and outside the empirical world. Not quite the Kantian view, since we need not be committed to empirical determinism, nor to saying that every event has a cause. But if we do not want to say that human action happens in a distinct noumenal world, where does it happen? Our problem is that we believe it can make a difference in the observable empirical world.

Human intervention enters into empirical causation when a cause is seen as a factor which can be produced or prevented, and thereby some event, the effect, be produced or prevented. In this approach, we are considering the results of our actual or possible interventions in the world. So, as von Wright put it,[27] 'To regard things as being causally related is the intellectual privilege of agents who think that they are free to interfere with the world.' This he calls a 'manipulative' or 'experimentalist' view of causation. It makes the notion of agency conceptually prior to that of causation. But von Wright also insists that it is not the action of interfering which is the cause; the cause is the state of affairs produced by the action. This is because the 'state of affairs' can be described as an event, and 'event causation' is distinguished from agency. If event causation is a conceptual presentation, different from the conceptual presentation of agency as such, the two can be kept distinct. But if we are to go behind conceptual distinctions to concrete happenings, these may form a complex of actions and natural processes, and we still have no satisfactory view of how causal relations hold within this complex. To quote von Wright again: 'In the idea of putting systems in motion the notions of action and causation meet.'[28] Here, we have the 'idea' and the 'notions' – a relation of concepts. But he also speaks of putting systems in motion as something we actually do. 'The discovery of causal relations presents two aspects: an active and a passive one. The active one is the putting in motion systems through producing their initial states. The passive is observing what happens inside the systems as far as possible without disturbing them.'[29] So we are said to 'produce an initial state, that sets a system in motion'.

If now we observe a regular sequence between two states of the world, and if one of the two is a state we can produce, then we may, by producing it, succeed in bringing about the other as well . . . If this turns out to be the case, we vest the first of these two states with a 'power' of producing the second state *analogous* to our power of producing the first. We then say that the first state is a *cause* of the second. But what this comes to, over and above a statement of regular sequence, is that if we *could* produce (could have produced) the first state on an occasion when it does (did) obtain, we should bring (have brought) about the second in consequence.[30]

Thus he refers us to our power to produce an initial state of affairs; when this state is followed by another, it is called a cause. But if 'power' is used of the cause-state, it goes into inverted commas. So important is it to remove the notion of 'power' from cause that if it appears where it might be allowed to be present, namely in our own ability to initiate states of affairs, then this is something different from causation.

So event causation gives trouble where at first sight we should least expect it – namely, in those views in which a cause is said to be a factor which by producing or preventing, we can produce or prevent some state of affairs said to be its effect. Collingwood, whose discussion of Causation[31] is the *locus classicus* of this view, makes a cause something we can produce or prevent, and by so doing produce or prevent something else. But the cause is the event or state of affairs we produce — not the producing of it. Von Wright, I have said, also insists that it is not the interfering or manipulating agent who is the cause, but some event which he has brought about.

> Causal relations exist between natural events, not between agents and events. When by *doing p* we *bring about q*, it is the *happening* of *p* which *causes q* to come. And *p* has this effect quite independently of whether it happens as a result of action or not. The *causal* relation is between *p* and *q*. The relation between the agent and the cause is different. The agent is not 'cause of the cause', but the cause *p* is the *result* of the agent's action.[32]

And, still more forcibly, he says that to speak of actions themselves as causes of their results is a '*bad* mistake'.[33] We were told that people started by thinking about causation in nature on analogy with their own actions. They could make things happen, so it was thought other happenings were caused by other kinds of agents. Agency was the original model of causation, and to extend this was called animistic superstition. To exorcise it Russell, in particular, tried to eliminate causation from science in favour of notions of law and functional dependence.[34] Now causation comes back, at any rate in the philosophical literature, in a form that eliminates agency.[35]

What then is this non-causal capacity to initiate states of affairs? It would almost seem that we are back into magic. We can make things happen by a fiat, which is itself outside the causal sequence. Or, if we are not stuck with magic, we may be stuck with the Kantian separation of phenomenal causation and noumenal freedom.

Yet agency is said to be a capacity to intervene effectively in the world. By intervening we can produce results. Some of these are unintentional, we might say accidental. I rush round the corner, barge into you, and knock you down. You say, I ought to have looked where I was going. I didn't look, and my bodily propulsion was no different (though perhaps less violent) than that of a runaway car. But suppose we are footballers, and I pull you down in a tackle. I knock you down 'on purpose', and there are rules as to how I may do it without fouling. What happens in both cases are movements of my body communicating movements to your body. If I am said to be an agent in doing this, either I have done it knowing what I was doing, and why; in the case of my barging into you I may be culpable, because, if I had thought what I was doing, I might have prevented myself from doing it. So we come to the difference between bodily movements which are vehicles or expressions of intentional actions, and those which are just happenings. The former also are happenings, and through them we have impacts on other things in the world. The account in terms of event causation cuts off these happenings and treats them as sequences of units. I have said that this loses transition and communication of movement. I have also said that by concentrating on what can properly be said about descriptions of events, it loses sight of them as real occurrences since descriptions in themselves are non-events. Now we have a view in which actions are excluded, and event causation leaves us with a world in which nothing interacts with anything else.

This need not be so if events are not basic causal units. We do indeed talk about event causation, but this is a shorthand for talking about transactions among their participants. My colliding with you caused your falling down; but it was *I* who collided with *you*. Certain events caused me to change my mind: that is to say that my taking note of what was happening provided me with a reason for changing my mind which I did not ignore. And if I say my noticing what was happening alarmed me, the noticing was something I did as a participant in the situation.

There can be an epistemology of causal explanation in which events enter as units. The explanations link statements in which events are edited under descriptions, and in this idiom we do of course speak of one event as causing another. But if we probe into the ontology behind the explanations, we come to participants whose doings and adventures are recorded in the descriptions of the events. If causes are operations of participants, some being persons and some physical things, this allows us to get actions back, as it were, into the act, and not be left with a dualism between causal sequences of events and actions outside them. If 'event causation' leads to this dualism, this is one of the troubles over event causation itself.

5 Actions

As H. A. Prichard said,[1] in acting, we 'butt into' the world, and look for differences which our butting in makes. This is particularly so when we are trying to detect causes. We think our actions make a difference to the 'course of events'. They make a difference primarily through our moving other things about. Not all movements are actions – my falling down is not an action but something I undergo, and which I experience from inside as something painful happening to me. Movements which are actions are experienced from inside as intentionally directed. What is experienced is not our willing bodily movements to take place, and then finding that they do (or perhaps don't). It is an experience of activity taking shape through bodily movements in a world in which we are also moved (this can be said independently of whether we take a determinist or indeterminist view of how these movements originate).

Actions, then, whatever else they are, are movements. Our experience as agents is one of moving ourselves, and thereby moving other things. Here I am glad to quote Davidson:[2] 'We must conclude, perhaps with a shock of surprise, that our primitive actions, the ones we do not do by doing something else, mere movements of the body – these are all the actions there are: the rest is up to nature.' I should demur over the word 'mere' if this means that actions are only neural and muscular movements. The movements called actions are movements of embodied persons, and traditionally causation has had a familiar use in speaking of these. (I think Davidson would accept this.)

To say that it had a familiar use in speaking about human actions is not to say that this does not have its problems. We all know that there are persistent questions about action: about 'the will', about motives, about what Prichard, in a now well-known phrase, called 'setting oneself to do' something,[3] and about what would count as the 'basic actions' to which one sets oneself. There are also the questions about actions as purposive, as done for reasons, and as to whether reasons are causes. There is a vast literature on all this; I shall only draw on it with the

42

particular, and I hope limited, concern of looking at action in relation to causation.

So what is the action, and where does it begin and end? Is it simply whatever it is that we directly do, or does it include what ensues from something we do directly? There are difficulties both ways; on the narrow view, there is the question of just what it is that we do directly; on the wider view, though it is not implausible to say that we have 'done' something which ensues from what we do (at any rate we can be held responsible for it), how far down the line should this bounding of the action go?

It can be bounded under different descriptions. Suppose I share a garden with you. I am digging a piece of ground to plant beans, and I go and dig up your carrot seeds. If asked 'What were you doing?', I could say (a) 'planting beans'. This could be narrowed down by saying I was (b) 'digging': (c) 'using a spade:' (d) 'moving my limbs:' (e) 'contracting my muscles:' (f) 'producing neural explosions in the brain.' Normally, I would describe what I was doing under (a) or (b), and if asked how I did it, I might give (c), and, if pressed further, perhaps (d), but I should be unlikely to go to (e) or (f), except as excursions into physiology. 'Digging' (b) could be called the core action, with (c), (d), (e) and (f) as means to (b); I am probably not aware of (e) except by a deliberate switch of attention, and almost certainly not aware of (f). If you tell me that what I have done is dig up your carrot seeds, this would normally be seen not as the action, but as its consequence, regrettable but unintended. I may nevertheless be responsible; I should, for instance, have consulted with you before I chose to dig that patch.

We may indeed be held responsible for unintended consequences, as in 'negligence' in the civil law, and in the 'absolute offence' in the criminal law. So though the description of the core action can be given by what we were presumably intending to do, the statement of what we did can be made wider where there is an interest in ascribing responsibility for consequences, though there has to be a limit, if not an obviously natural limit, somewhere. There is a nursery jingle:

> For want of a nail
> The shoe was lost;
> For want of a shoe
> The horse was lost;
> For want of a horse
> The rider was lost;
> For want of a rider

> The battle was lost;
> For want of a battle
> The kingdom was lost;
> And all for the want
> Of a horse-shoe nail.

The moral is supposed to be that carelessness in small matters can have far-reaching consequences. To extend responsibility so far for what one has done is harsh; though one might perhaps go as far as the loss of the horse. To extend it further seems not only harsh, but wildly implausible. The outcome of the battle probably depended on a number of factors, and the loss of one rider is unlikely to have been a sufficient single factor to have produced such a result. Single strand causation is being imposed on a situation which is a complex network of happenings. And if the result of the battle could be said to have turned on the loss of one particular rider (perhaps he was the general), we might go on pressing consequences of negligence over the nail even beyond the loss of the kingdom – and if so, how much further? We must surely stop somewhere; the further we go on into perpetuity, the greater the ramifications of one strand with others.

Widening and narrowing of the description of the action has been called the 'accordion effect' by J. Feinberg.[4] When the action is drawn out, it can include consequences for which we are held responsible. When it is being pushed in more narrowly, this may be seen as an attempt to fasten on what it is, in a strict sense, that we actually and directly do. How far back can that go, and can it end with something we just do, without having to do something else as a means to it – with what has been called a 'basic action?'

The notion of basic actions was introduced by Arthur Danto;[5] an action B is basic if there is no other action A performed such that B is caused by A. This was refined in a later paper[6] by saying that, taking causation to be a relation between pairs of events, no event happens before a basic action so as to cause it.

Later writers on 'basic actions' have simplified the definitions by calling basic actions those which are not done by doing something else.[7] Then is the basic action something inside us that we just do? Let us look more closely at the 'accordion' with its wider and narrower descriptions of actions. If we try to chase actions further and further back into things happening inside us, we shall be speaking of things of which we are unaware. This is because our bodies normally act as instruments of our performances, without our having to worry about how they do it.

Writers in the literature then call attention to the possibility of a person's body, or part of it, not functioning – for example the paralysed limb. We might then say the action was frustrated. Normally, we describe an action under some overt change in the external world, and we do not think about the bodily means, except in the cases where these fail to function, as in paralysis. But there are times where attention to some part of the body and making it function can occupy the whole of one's attention and become the core action. This may happen in cases of extreme exhaustion. Antoine de Saint-Exupéry knew well such situations.[8] In describing flying alone in an appalling storm over the sea, he says that he was 'emptied of everything except the vision of a very simple act. I must straighten out, straighten out, straighten out'. But then it was not even this.

One has a pair of hands and they obey. How are one's orders transmitted to one's hands?

I had made a discovery which horrified me: my hands were numb. My hands were dead. They sent me no message. Probably they had been numb a long time and I had not noticed it. The pity was that I had noticed it, had raised the question. That was serious.

Lashed by the wind, the wings of the plane had been dragging and jerking at the cables by which they were controlled from the stick, and the stick in my hands had not ceased jerking a single second. I had been gripping the stick with all my might for forty minutes, fearful lest the strain snap the cables. So desperate had been my grip that now I could not feel my hands.

What a discovery! My hands were not my own. I looked at them and decided to lift a finger: it obeyed me. I looked away and issued the same order: now I could not feel whether the finger had obeyed or not. No message had reached me. I thought: 'Suppose my hands were to open: how would I know it?' I swung my head round and looked again: my hands were still locked round the wheel. Nevertheless, I was afraid. How can a man tell the difference between the sight of a hand opening and the decision to open that hand, when there is no longer an exchange of sensations between the hand and the brain? How can one tell the difference between an image and an act of the will? Better stop thinking of the picture of open hands. Hands live a life of their own. Better not offer them this monstrous temptation. And I began to chant a silly litany which went on uninterruptedly until this flight was over. A single thought. A single image. A single phrase tirelessly chanted over and over again: 'I shut my hands. I shut my hands. I shut my hands.' All of me was condensed into that phrase and for me the white sea, the whirling eddies, the saw-toothed range ceased to exist. There was only 'I shut my hands.' There was no danger, no cyclone, no land unattained. Somewhere there was a pair of rubber hands which, once they let go the wheel, could not possibly come alive in time to recover from the tumbling drop into the sea.

And again, of a friend, Guillaumet, struggling to base through the snow after having to ground his plane in the mountains: 'What saves a man is to take a step. Then another step. It is always the same step.' Then he finds his heart conking. 'I stayed still and listened to myself. Never, never in my life have I listened as carefully to a motor as I listened to my heart, me hanging there. I said to it, "Come on, old boy. Go to work. Try beating a little." That's good stuff my heart is made of. I hesitated, but it went on. You don't know how proud I was of that heart.'⁹

The intentional action is pushed to a very small span. Some transcendental meditators tell us it can be pushed still further, not only in conditions of extreme stress, but of extreme relaxation, and one can be conscious of and control what is going on in the body below the level of normal awareness. Be this as it may, my concern is with whether we can press back until we come to a basic action which can be an ultimate starter. There have been two candidates for starters. One has been that they are certain neurological events in the brain. We are certainly not aware of these starting up and triggering off further actions. Nevertheless (see the claims of the transcendental meditators) we cannot perhaps set an absolute limit to what we might be able to become aware of as going on inside us. More seriously, there is no satisfactory account of how actions under intentional descriptions correlate with actions seen as events which are instances of neurological laws. So chasing a basic action back to a neural event in the brain does not help to say how the action under an intentional description causes this event; we have a description of what is happening in terms of events, and the notion of an action need not come in.

Another candidate for a triggerer is to look for a basic action which is unequivocally an action, something which we do intentionally. This has been said to be an 'act of will', or 'volition'. 'Acts of will', or 'volitional acts' have had a bad press in recent philosophies of mind, and for good reasons. For one thing, we are not aware of performing an act of will to move our arm – we are aware of moving our arm, albeit in a manner we can characterise by an adverb. We move it voluntarily; the adverb describes a manner of doing the action, not a prior action which is its cause.[10] Moreover, if every action has to have a prior action as its cause, so that we have first to will and then move our arm, we should then have to will to will . . .

We can try to stop the regress by not making the act of will an event in a chain of events, where 'every event has a cause', including this one. It is not an evident axiom that 'every event has a cause', and there is no reason for stipulating it. However, if the act of will is not an initial event, but something we *do* to trigger off a chain of events, starting with physiological events, there is the difficulty of interaction between things of such different kinds. Even if we do not have to say that they belong to different types, so that their interaction would be a category mistake, and even if 'like can only be caused by like' is not an evident axiom, there is still the difficulty that if acts of will are causes of neural events, how is this sequence observed? The brain surgeon might observe neural events, but could not observe acts of will. The agent might (possibly) say he could observe an act of will introspectively, but he could not observe the neural events. But do we in fact have introspective knowledge of acts of will? Moreover, if the connection is a causal one, it is said that it should be possible to find a general law. What is this? 'All acts of will are followed by neural events'? If neural events come in, their law will be a physiological one. So Davidson says that if there were laws through which there could be causal explanations of psycho—physiological happenings, they would be physiological or even physical laws; and we do not know what they are.[11] This dilemma comes from holding that if acts of agents are acts of volition and these are causal they must come within the pattern of causal explanation which is held for event causation, and this they do not do.

Nevertheless, we may still want to look for a triggerer. If neither a neural event in the brain, nor a distinct act of will will fill the bill, is there any other candidate?

I have already mentioned one such, suggested by Prichard in 'Duty and Ignorance of Fact' as 'setting oneself' to do something.[12] This is, I think, a better candidate than the 'act of will'. It is a recognisable state to be in, especially when one has to bring oneself, or hold oneself, to something difficult. Saint-Exupéry set himself to concentrate on holding the stick in his hands, and his Guillaumet concentrated on taking the next step, and even on keeping his heart beating. Even where there is no such painful effort, there is some degree (it may only be a small one) of rousing oneself. The reflexive here can be significant. There is not something in us causing something else in us, but something that we ourselves are doing with ourselves. If this is to be specified as a basic action, it might be expressed through an internal accusative – like doing a deed, fighting a fight. An internal accusative is of course merely a linguistic device, but behind it lurks a suggestion of internal causation. (I shall be looking at this later in considering 'immanent causation'.)

'Setting oneself to' is, then, a possible candidate so long as it can be something we ourselves are doing with ourselves, not a particular event in an internal chain. If, however, it is to be brought as a cause within the scheme of causal explanation as a relation between events, it would have to be represented in the latter way. This comes out, I think, in Jennifer Hornsby's *Actions*, where she displaces Prichard's 'setting oneself to' by 'trying'. For her, trying is an internal event which is a cause of bodily movements, and is a basic action which I do not do by doing something else. Indeed, it is *the* action, everything else, including bodily movements, being its result or results. Miss Hornsby holds that actions, as tryings, are identified by their effects. My action in raising my arm is described transitively as my raising my arm. If my arm just rose because someone pushed it up, I should not describe it as an action. So an action is a person's trying, and it is specified by its effects.

What if the result is not what we were trying to do? Can we both say that actions are tryings and that they are specified by their effects?. Where these are unsuccessful, there is a gap between what we tried to do and what we actually did. Miss Hornsby has an example:

What is it though to try to act in some way?

Sometimes it is to act in some other way. Jane tries to return a service at tennis, and hits the ball into the net. One thing she did was try to hit the ball, and another thing she did was hit it into the net. But it is not that one has to do first the one thing and then the other in such cases, that having tried to hit the ball over the net (having had a shot at it), one then has to mitigate one's failure to get it over the net by now hitting it into the net. Having attempted ineptly to hit the ball over the net, one has already done all that one needs to do to have hit it into the net. One's trying to return it is one's hitting it into the net.

It seems that matters cannot be otherwise if one succeeds in doing exactly what was attempted. If someone's trying to hit the ball somewhere can be the same as his hitting it elsewhere, then his actually hitting it where he meant to could scarcely be different from his trying to hit it there. One thing that is done then is try to ϕ, and another thing that is done is ϕ. But having made a movement that is an attempt at ϕ-ing, no further doing is called for from the agent if he is to have ϕ-d. His attempt is then a success.[13]

Jane's hitting the ball into the net may indeed be the unhappy result of
her trying to return it, and if the action is the trying, and if it is known by
its results, one would then have to say her trying to return it was her
hitting it into the net, and indeed this is one action and not two. But if we
were explaining to a visitor who had never seen tennis played what Jane
was trying to do, one would tell him that she was trying to get it over the
net, and past her opponent and perhaps down the side line. Here
the account of what it means to 'return the ball' is an intentional one.
The difference is between a description of the action that took place, and
its explanation under an intentional description. (This can go with Miss
Hornsby's saying that to try to act in some way is sometimes to act in
another way.)

Under an intentional description,[14] 'trying' implies having an objective which in this case was not achieved. Under the description of the
action that took place, this action was indeed, as Miss Hornsby says,
hitting the ball into the net, and this was the effect of Jane's trying to
return the ball. But what she was trying to do is made intelligible by
reference to something which did not take place – getting the ball over
the net. Unsuccessful actions can be described by effects, when we are
describing what happened. Yes: but if they are 'tryings', they need also
to be described by reference to an intention, and then we see the point of
calling them unsuccessful. The difficulty is in combining three requirements: (1) that trying is an internal event which causes other events;
(2) that a trying, as an action, is identified by its effects; and (3) that
actions can also be specified under intentional descriptions. So if we ask
(a) 'What did Jane do?' and (b) 'What was Jane trying to do?' the answer
to (a) could be 'hit the ball into the net', and to (b) 'return the ball':
(b) can be substituted for (a) only by disregarding an ambiguity in 'return',
which is indicated by saying she returned the ball 'ineptly'. She returned
the ball ineptly, but it would not make sense to say she was trying to
return the ball ineptly. She was trying to return it good and proper, over
the net. So 'trying', and I think also 'return', are applicable to actions
under intentional descriptions, where they refer to objectives which may
not be achieved.

Miss Hornsby then gives another example, where what John was
trying to do, though he didn't succeed, is inferred from what he is
observed to do.

'He tried to turn on the light by flicking the switch.'

Suppose that John does try to turn on the light by flicking the
switch, but that the bulb has gone. A spectator who knew that the

bulb had gone and who disbelieved that John would succeed in turning on the light may have known that John, in his ignorance, would at least try to turn it on. He could take his flicking the switch as proof that he tried to turn it on. And it seems that he has his proof because John's switch flicking was his trying to turn on the light. But if (by § 2.1) flicking the switch was something else that John tried to do, and yet John did not make two attempts at getting the light on, then there was only one (variously describable) trying on his part. Thus his switch flicking must equally be his trying to flick the switch. His succeeding in ϕ-ing is his trying to ϕ.[15]

Here, the spectator is allowed to have information which enables him to infer what the agent was trying to do. If one imagines a spectator without background information, for instance, one unfamiliar with the game of tennis, to explain to him what the player was trying to do one would have to give a description of what it is to return a ball successfully. In this case this would be a description of an objective which was not achieved, and not a description of the effects which were observed. Observed effects are clues to tryings, but are not sufficient to specify them. Specification of an intentional action calls for more information than specification by results. Generally this information is taken for granted, so the result is at once recognised as successful or unsuccessful. But this need not be so.

To look for chains of events going back to an event which is a trigger cause and also an internal act is to make the action an event within a chain of events, and it ends by losing agent causation. Miss Hornsby wants 'tryings' to be basic actions which are internal events. An action, she says, is a cause, which is identified by its results, and the results are events which are then followed by other events. So how does the action of the agent get into the story of events as causally related to other events?

Davidson is very aware of this difficulty:

We explain a broken window by saying that a brick broke it: what explanatory power the remark has derives from the fact that we may first expand the account of the cause to embrace an event, the movement of the brick, and we can then summon up evidence for the existence of a law connecting such events as motions of medium-sized rigid objects and the breaking of windows. The ordinary notion of cause is inseparable from this elementary form of explanation. But the concept of agent causation lacks these features entirely. What distinguishes agent causation from ordinary causation is that no expansion into a tale of two events is possible, and no law lurks. By the same token, nothing is explained. There seems no good reason, therefore, for using such expressions, as 'cause', 'bring about', 'make the case' to *illuminate* the relation between an agent and his act. I do not mean that there is anything wrong with such expressions – there are times when they come naturally in talk of agency. But I do not think that by introducing them we make any progress towards understanding agency and action.

Causality is central to the concept of agency, but it is ordinary causality between events that is relevant, and it concerns the effects and not the causes of actions (discounting, as before, the possibility of analysing intention in terms of causality).[16]

The exclusion (at any rate *pro hac vice*) of analysis of intention as causation underlines the fact that what is being said here is that if agency does not fit into event causation, then it is doubtful whether it is helpful to speak of agency causation except as a practical *façon de parler*. It may indeed be an unavoidable one, but, according to Davidson in the passage quoted, 'nothing is thereby explained'. This is assuming that causal explanation must be in terms of what he calls 'ordinary causality between events'. I have questioned whether causation is indeed a relation between events. Be this as it may, the 'nomic subsumption' model of explanation, where a singular event is an instance of a general law, need not be the only kind of explanation. Taking explanation as an answer to a 'Why' question that gives intellectual satisfaction, different kinds of answer may be appropriate in different contexts. If I ask 'Why did you open that window?' a reply 'Because I noticed a gas leak' can be taken as a sufficient explanation. It gives a reason for the action. (On the view of pure event causation, reasons would be epiphenomenal, or what is now called 'supervenient'; they would have no causal role.)

Explanation by reasons has traditionally been called 'teleological'. Nowadays philosophers more often speak of acting from intentions. This may be an improvement, 'teleological' suggesting an end pulling from in front, whereas there is an objective entertained in the present, and one takes steps intentionally to implement it. The steps are intelligible to an observer if he knows the objective for which they are taken. If it is said that it is circular to give an explanation of the action in terms of intention, where it has already been described by a word used for intentional actions, one could reply that this is the explanation which makes what was being done intelligible.

So we have some actions explained through intentions. Intentions need not be introspectable mental events. They get expression in actions which are bodily movements made intelligible when they are presented as intentionally directed. I push you aside, and I explain what I was doing by saying that I was not just colliding with you, but was pushing you out of the way of an approaching car.[17] 'Pushing you out of the way' is a description under an intention, whereas 'colliding with you' is not, although the net result might be the same (apart perhaps from the possibility of your thanking me).

In her book *Intention*[18] Miss Anscombe has brought out how 'intentional' refers to a form of description. She was, I think, the first to introduce the term of 'under a description' which is now widely accepted in the literature. In her paper 'Under a description'[19] she traces the ancestry of this to Aristotle's way of presenting something *as* something (ἡ or in Latin *qua*).

When events are described under intentions, they are seen as doings and not just as happenings. Not all doings, of course, are intentional; most of them are not. Some philosophers have made a distinction by calling unintentional ones 'acts' and intentional ones 'actions'. I think this is difficult to sustain, and I hope that it is clear in context when I am speaking of actions as intentional doings, and when I am speaking of what people (or other things) can do unintentionally.

What the description of the action under an intention gives us is not a final cause as operating from the future, but the action as a step or steps taken to an objective entertained in the present. If an action is directed towards an objective, it may or may not succeed in obtaining or achieving it. Hence the difficulty of fitting actions under intentional descriptions into event causation. Davidson thinks this would have to be done by specifying them through beliefs and desires, which can be events. But there is no law correlating these with the events which are said to be their results, or with possible underlying physiological events which might be said to be their causes. So actions are not explained on a model of event causation which looks for instances of general laws. Davidson accepts that we need to talk about agency causation in terms of intention; his qualms are over its theoretical propriety. There is a problem too in identifying what would be the basic unit in an action as a cause. Davidson holds that any action as described through an intention could be basic – he says 'primitive' – because it is a unit as the action under that description. I opened a window. Under that intentional description of what I did, I do not have to say I set going a neural mechanism which caused me to move my hands which had the effect of my opening the window. Yet of course I opened the window through making bodily movements. The movements give effect to the action; and our bodily movements are movements among those of other bodies in a common world. The movements which give effect to our actions produce results in movements of other things. At least, this is intuitively what we believe happens. Common sense intuition can, however, be reinforced by explanatory usefulness; in actions, we 'butt into' the world, and one of the most prevalent forms of causal explanation comes by noticing the differences our butting in makes. We explain our butting in by referring to what we intend or expect to be its results in the external world. Why must the 'results' not be allowed to be 'effects'? Only, it would seem, because causation has been decreed to be event causation. If intentional actions cannot be fitted into a model of event causation, this may be because all causation is not event causation. Indeed, I should go further, since I have queried whether any of it is. Event causation may indeed be presented as one model of causal explanation, showing an event as an instance of a law-like regularity. But going on in the world behind this presentation are the actions and reactions of the participants in the event, and this is where I should look for causation. Some of the participants are human agents, and why need their doings be excluded from the causal story? Indeed, the old view which saw our actions as the paradigm example of causation was not so wrong; it was only wrong in supposing that the actions and reactions of other things must also turn them into agents.

The notion of cause is more complex than appears in the nomic subsumption view. One feature of this complexity is the difficulty of isolating single-strand linear sequences from the network of what may be other necessary conditions within which the 'effect' occurs. And some of these may be human actions.

6 Causes as Select Factors

There is a well-known passage in J. S. Mill's discussion of Causation[1] where he says:

> Nothing can better show the absence of any scientific ground for the distinction between the cause of a phenomenon and its conditions than the capricious manner in which we select from among the conditions that which we choose to denominate the cause. However numerous the conditions may be, there is hardly any of them which may not, according to the purpose of our immediate discourse, obtain that nominal pre-eminence.

This, he says, has no 'scientific propriety'. If, to 'select from the conditions that which we choose to denominate the cause' means that this choice is 'capricious', and lacks 'scientific propriety', what is the alternative? For if we say that selection is unjustified and that all antecedent conditions must be included, we may have to end with the total preceding state of the universe. So Bridgman says in *The Logic of Modern Physics*[2] that 'We do not have a simple event *A* causally connected with a single event *B*, but the whole background of the system in which the events occur is included in the concept and is a vital part of it.' But if the whole background of the system is included in the concept, the concept of Cause becomes quite unusable. Those who take the cause in this way may in the end say it is the whole state of the universe, and no one can give an account of this.

Bridgman may of course be taking 'the system in which the events occur' in a more limited sense than the whole universe, but if we press the reference to 'the whole background' we may in the end not be able to stop short of this.[3] The whole state of the universe may indeed be the background of whatever happens. But mercifully we do not have to go into this to produce more restricted causal explanations, both in science and in everyday life. Does this restriction only give the factors selected as causes what Mill calls 'nominal pre-eminence'?

54

If we select one condition in a state of affairs and call it the cause of an ensuing condition, described as the effect, there may and very likely will be, a gap between the condition cited as cause and that cited as effect, and the gap will be occupied by other necessary conditions. The cause of the explosion was that a lighted cigarette-end had been dropped. There may have been a considerable interval between the dropping of the cigarette-end and the trail of fire along the floor reaching the place where certain chemicals were stored. But an inquiry into the cause of the explosion would want to know what happened that might have been prevented. So the citing of a cause in this sense is not an attempt to give a total account of all necessary and sufficient conditions; still less (*per impossible*) of the whole preceding state of the universe. It works by citing one factor out of a complex of conditions.

A view of how this selection might be made and justified was put by R. G. Collingwood in his now well-known discussion of Cause.[4] He distinguished three senses of Cause. First, where it is used in a historical context, in speaking of what caused someone to act as he did, and where it refers to something in the situation or in the behaviour of other people which provided the person with a motive for so acting. Here 'cause' is assimilated to 'reason', where there is a belief on the agent's part that a situation is of a certain character, plus a desire to do something about it, and a belief that a certain course of action will be appropriate.[5] The second is the use of 'cause' in practical life and in the experimental sciences, where it is an event or state of things which is within our power to produce or prevent, and by producing or preventing it, we can produce or prevent that event or state of things of which it is said to be the cause. The third sense is where what is caused is an event or state of things, and the cause is another event or state of things standing in a one-to-one relation, such that if the cause happens the effect must also happen, even if no further conditions are fulfilled, and the effect cannot happen without the cause. This third sense, Collingwood says, has little theoretical power. What has power is his second sense, where, in practical life and experimental science, it can be shown that by producing and preventing one state of affairs another is produced or prevented. So the fire was caused by the dropping of a lighted cigarette: the aeroplane crash was caused by metal fatigue which had not been detected and dealt with. This justifies the selection of one factor, namely one which could have been removed. I have already noted that von Wright has a similar view.[6] Causation depends on action; the characteristic way of testing it is experiment, which is a form of action, especially of manipulative action. Experimental action has a conditional and counterfactual aspect; it is looking for a change which will not occur unless we produce it, or which did not occur because we did not produce it. So 'to regard things as being causally related is the intellectual privilege of agents who think they are free to interfere with the world.'

The possibility of practical intervention has as one of its background conditions a world containing human beings who can so intervene. Since they will need motives for doing so, such a view will relate statements of cause to human interests and purposes. These will not only be interests in producing or preventing states of affairs for practical ends. They may be theoretical interests, to understand how something works by manipulating it, or indeed imagining how it might work in a thought experiment. Thus enquiries into 'the cause of cancer' may be of intellectual interest as bearing on the understanding of the division of cells and how this is controlled in the body, or it may be motivated by the hope that it may be possible to isolate a factor, perhaps the activity of a virus, and that this activity might be counteracted. Probably in most medical research, the motivation (and no doubt the funding) comes from both kinds of interest. But though the interest or motive may be seen as a sociological fact about why people study the problem, its solution can be an intellectual achievement. Moreover, the practical and theoretical concern may be differently weighted; the practical interest can be in the forefront, to produce or prevent some state of affairs for some end, or the interest may be to find out more about natural processes, with experiments to test hypotheses about them.

The reference to 'thought experiments' indicates that the condition to be selected as causal need not, as Collingwood held, be one actually produced or prevented by human interference. Rather, it should be possible to imagine a state of affairs in which other conditions could remain constant while this one was absent. One way in which this may be done is by comparing the situation in which an event to be called the 'effect' occurs (the 'effect-situation') with others like it in causally relevant respects in which it does not occur ('comparison-situations'). We then identify the condition which differentiates the effect-situation from the comparison-situations. The phrase 'causally relevant respects' may seem to beg a question – or perhaps two questions, in the word 'causally' and in the word 'relevant'. I shall come back to this. The immediate point is that by means of the comparison, one condition can be distinguished from others which can be called 'background conditions'. Raymond Martin, who has written about this view,[7] takes the example of a barn burning down as an effect-situation, and as comparison-situations other barns similarly constructed which have not burnt down. The differentiating condition might be that the former was struck by lightning. This would be a fairly obvious and non-controversial cause. Where Martin's view gets interesting is that he imagines an effect-situation in which the barn which burnt down had been built as the result of a directive in somebody's will, which was not the case with any of those in the comparison-situations. Why is this not cited as a possible cause? To say that the directive is 'causally irrelevant' would, as I have suggested, beg the question, and Martin does not just say this. He says the differentiating condition called 'causal' must involve some portion of a temporal state prior to the state in which the effect occurred. Here this would be the barn being struck by lightning as prior to its burning down. Could 'being built in accordance with a directive in a will' describe such a prior state? Why is it not thought to be the relevant one to select as a cause?

In a society where witchcraft accusations are rife, it might be thought to be just this. The relatives of the dead man put a curse on the barn because of the directive to build it which took the money they expected to inherit under the will. In a society where witchcraft was taken seriously, a local sceptic might try to find other barns built in accordance with such directives, and cursed and not burnt down, so as to find appropriate comparison-situations. If it be said that the differentiating factor is not the directive but the curse, then the fact that the curse was put on because of the directive makes the latter a factor relevant to the occurrence of the fire. The relevance would be due to a background system of beliefs into which the generalisation that curses can cause fires fits. And if this relevance is to be challenged, the belief system must be challenged.

I have introduced the word 'factor' here and in the title of this chapter, whereas the more common word in the literature is 'condition'. Discussions turn on whether a condition is a necessary one, and what combination of conditions would be sufficient. *Pace* Mill, it is generally conceded that it is impossible to cite all the conditions, and that to give a cause, a selection has to be made. The word 'factor' is, I think, a stronger word to use in a causal context than 'condition'. A factor is defined in the OED as 'an element that enters into the composition of anything', and mathematically as 'one or two or more numbers which when multiplied together produce a given number'. Here the order in which they are taken is irrelevant; factors can be extracted from a composition, and certainly from a mathematical sum, *ex post facto*. In the case of *causal* factors, the metaphors in 'enter into' and 'produce' (if they are metaphors) are stronger, and suggest priority. There is also a suggestion of agency in the original meaning of 'factor'; I am not raising this here, but taking 'factor' more widely as something which contributes to the happening of something else. To speak of a 'factor' excludes this as being a total cause; it may nevertheless be appropriately given as a cause.

To say *x* was the cause of *y* is, then, to give *x* pre-eminence over other conditions in explaining why *y* occurred, but this is not, as Mill called it, only 'nominal-pre-eminence'. It can be argued, in the ways I have indicated, that it is the condition that names a factor relevant to what we want to explain. This can vary with the description of the situation, and which features in it are emphasised in each description. Take the spread of an influenza epidemic. Its cause, as an *influenza* epidemic, could be given by the pathologist as the incidence of a particular virus. Seen as the spread of an influenza *epidemic* it could be ascribed by the public health authorities as due to people crowding together in public places like cinemas. The cause for its spreading *now* might be given by the weather-men as due to an unseasonably mild spell of weather. Why it reached this country at all might be ascribed to the arrival of a group of sailors from Hong Kong. All these accounts may be true; which factor is named as cause and which factors as contributory conditions may be, as General Haig would say 'contextualized'. I owe this word to Alistair Cooke's remarks in a 'Letter from America'[8] speaking of how Mr Alexander Haig might respond to statements on defence by a Cabinet colleague. Since, under the American system he was not bound by collective responsibility, he might have said, 'Go to hell', but Alistair Cooke says he wouldn't, because having been brought up in the Pentagon, he uses words of four or five syllables, and makes up some, like 'contextualize'. (Having said this, I wish also to put on record my respect for Mr Haig.)

So a factor is selected and its prominence can be argued for according to context. This is why any given cause is only a partial explanation, and talk about necessary and sufficient conditions is no substitute for talking about causes. It is no substitute because all the necessary conditions would be too many to list. J. L. Mackie tried to defend the selection of one by defining a cause as an *insufficient* but *necessary* part of a condition which is in itself *unnecessary* but *sufficient* for the result,[9] calling this an INUS condition. So a short circuit formed a necessary but insufficient part of a condition in itself unnecessary, but which was then sufficient for a fire to break out. To name *x* as an INUS condition, it should be possible to imagine it as absent. It need not actually be produced or prevented, provided the difference its absence would make can be imagined. To imagine the absence of *x* in a thought experiment, would be a step towards testing the suggestion that it is an INUS condition.

The definition of cause as an INUS condition (insufficient but necessary part of a condition which is unnecessary but sufficient for the result) raises the question of whether there is a unique condition which can be so described. In Mackie's example, a short circuit was an INUS condition for starting the fire; other conditions, such as the presence of inflammable material were also necessary, but would not have been sufficient of themselves without the short circuit, and the short circuit need not have occurred. But it might have occurred, and still not have started a fire if there had not been foam rubber lying around, and the foam rubber need not have been lying around. A sufficient condition is only sufficient given other conditions which are necessary; in the whole complex of conditions more than one can be quoted not only as a *conditio sine qua non*, but as one which, given the other conditions, completes the state of affairs sufficient for the 'effect'. So we come back to the question of selection. The selection can be made by asking what factor in the state of affairs might be produced or prevented, either in practice or in a thought experiment. If several of the conditions could have been produced or prevented, which one we go for can depend on the interest through which the state of affairs is approached (as in the instance, given above, of the spread of an influenza epidemic). In his later views on causation in *The Cement of the Universe*,[10] Mackie allows different conditions in different contexts (which he calls 'causal fields') to count as INUS conditions.

I see no problem here in allowing what is called 'over-determination'; given background conditions, any one of two or more operative factors could have been sufficient for the effect. A man might have a fatal heart attack just as he was shot through the head. M. Bunzl in a paper 'Causal Overdetermination' says that in such cases one of these must in fact get in first, and pre-empt the other as cause.[11] This, I think, assumes a hard-line causal chain, not a network of factors. On the latter view, I see no reason why either of two operating at the same time might not have been sufficient for the effect.

Hart and Honoré, in *Causation in the Law*,[12] show that in the law, interest in citing a cause will be to look for something abnormal or untoward in a state of affairs which will include a number of other conditions which may also be contributory. The cause which is the factor so selected need not be in immediate temporal contiguity with the effect. A recent example is the judgement given in the Appeal Court in two cases (*Regina v. Malcherek* and *Regina v. Steel*)[13] where women had been gravely injured in assaults and had been put on life-support machines. The doctors had in each case decided that there was complete cessation of brain function and accordingly switched off the machine. The juries in the trials had been instructed not to consider the question of causation. The submissions in the appeals were that the doctors, by switching off the ventilator and life-support machines, were the cause of death, or, more accurately, that there was evidence, which the jury should have been allowed to consider, that the doctors, and not the assailant in each case might have been the cause of death. The judges, in dismissing the appeal, in so far as it related to the issue of causation, held that in either case the original wound or injury was 'a continuing operating and substantial cause' of the death of the victim, and the intervention of medical treatment (which in the judgement of the doctors could no longer serve any useful purpose) did not exonerate the original assailant for responsibility for the death.

In an earlier case (*Rex v. Smith*, 1959) Lord Parker had said:

It seems to the court that if at the time of death the original wound is still an operating cause and a substantial cause, then the death can properly be said to be the result of the wound, albeit that some other cause of death is also operating . . . Only if the second cause is so overwhelming as to make the original wound merely part of the history can it be said that the death does not flow from the wound.

In legal, or quasi-legal contexts, factors cited as causes can be and often are acts of omission. If one then asks how something which did not happen can cause something to happen, this is because the interest is in assigning responsibility,[14] or in thinking how something could have been otherwise, or it is in both. In other words, this is a natural field for counterfactual conditionals: 'if *x* had not happened, *y* would not have happened'; or 'if *x* had happened, *y* would not have happened' . . . and the like. This is often the form taken in inquiries into causes of disasters. A report in *The Times* of 26 July 1980 of an Irish Government inquiry into a disaster, in which the Belgium tanker *Betelgeuse* blew up in Bantry Bay killing 50 people, is a string of counterfactuals. If the ship had not been allowed to become corroded, the structure would not have buckled. If there had been equipment on board capable of calculating stress due to incorrect ballasting, the hull would not have been weakened. If the man who should have been at his post as despatcher in the control room had not been missing, alarm could have been given and lives saved. Had the man who was acting as despatcher observed the disaster at the beginning, it is probable that lives could have been saved. If the company had maintained the standby tug close to the jetty, it is probable that the lives of the jetty crew would have been saved despite the absence of the control room despatcher. Had the company provided suitable escape craft, it was probable that the victims on the jetty and the ship would have been saved.

Here the interest is clearly that of assigning responsibility. Physical causes of the explosion will also have been investigated, but there does not appear to have been agreement on these (the company recorded its view that the tanks exploded as a result of a fire which it believed started on the jetty). Whatever the immediate physical causes, the main concern of the inquiry was to find the circumstances in which they operated, so as to apportion responsibility by looking for factors which could be connected with human agency.

The connection can, as in this report, be with what people failed to do. Acts of omission give causal explanations in an indirect way, *via* subjunctive counterfactuals: if x had done y, z would have happened, *ergo y* would have caused z. Since this cannot always be established with certainty, the conclusion that z would have happened may have to be given as only likely (as in some of the conclusions in this report). The point, however, is that an act of omission can be cited as a cause indirectly through an implicit reference to a causal statement of what would (or probably would) have happened had the omitted act occurred. So in allowing acts of omission to be causes, in this indirect sense, I am not going back on saying that a cause is efficacious in producing an effect. The cause by omission rests on the presumption that if some one had done something, it would have been efficacious in making something else happen. Causal statements, especially in practical and experimental situations, are not just reports of what is observed to occur; they can be made through suppositions of what would occur or have occurred were some factor to be different, or had it been different.

This shows a complexity in the notion of cause, especially in connecting physical happenings with the actions and omissions of human agents, and where assigning causes by selecting factors is directed by an interest in ascribing responsibility by noting what human agents did or failed to do. It is sometimes said that the notion of cause is properly at home where there is a reference to human interests, and here it is serviceable in spite of being a comparatively blunt instrument. Where precision tools are needed, it is likely to be replaced by notions of functional dependence or law.

There is some force in this; but it cannot, I think, be the whole story. In practical and experimental contexts, people can interfere with the course of nature and the results of their interference be noted. However, interference is only effective because there is in some sense a course of nature. This need not be a reign of iron determinism (indeed it pretty certainly is not, since if it were how could we make deliberate interferences?). But it is a world in which some conditions remain constant while we interfere with others; otherwise we could not predict the probable outcome of our interference. For this, we need to know not only what are standing conditions, but also something about the general ways in which they 'stand'. Our particular interventions thus presuppose a background when things happen in regular ways and we give causal explanations which presuppose generalisations about what is likely to happen when people do this kind of thing. When agents intervene in states of affairs there is a tacit, if not explicit, assumption that there are persisting regularities which enable the results of their actions to be not just haphazard. So where a particular cause in a particular situation is selected by picking on some factor that can be produced or prevented by human agency, this is only part of the story. The story has to be filled out by connecting the notion of cause with a background of generalisations.[15] Some of the generalisations may be rules of thumb; some may be dignified by being called laws of nature.

'Laws of nature' I take not just to be directives to be followed in investigating nature. Neither do I take them to be 'nomic necessities', nor 'universals of fact' in the sense of merely empirical generalisations.[16] They are universals of facts, but with a theoretical formulation which enables them to support conditionals about what may be found to happen. Their status as laws comes from their being high-level generalisations in theories from which lower-level generalisations can be deduced and empirically tested.[17] They are generalisations supporting predictions about how natural processes will be found to be; and their connection with other laws in scientific theories makes expectations based on them carry more weight that if they were only inductive generalisations drawn from how natural processes have already been found to be. Nevertheless, they do formulate general properties in natural processes, and in this sense are universals of fact. These general properties, especially those described in the laws of physics, will underlie other properties (which is not saying that other properties can be reduced to them), and they put constraints on what can happen, nature being like this (which is not saying that they determine what will happen). The temptation to call them 'necessary' comes from these constraints, but there need not have been these particular constraints.

Moreover, new laws may evolve, and we do not know how far back into nature evolution may extend.

The distinction between laws of nature and more restricted causal laws is not an absolute one, but there are differences in scope of generality. Causal explanations are unlikely to invoke the most general physical laws of nature. The cause of why a building collapsed would not be likely to be said to be the Law of Gravity, however much this was a background condition. It would, for example, be said to have been caused by cracks in the foundations produced by subsidence due to mining operations. Moreover, except in the ideal case, a law of nature does not show what happens except in conjunction with other factors. Gravity may combine with other countervailing forces, as in propulsion or in air currents. Sometimes the total resultant is calculable, as in ballistics; sometimes not, as in the fall of a leaf. Causes are selected from detailed complexes of conditions, and some of these complexes are unlikely to recur. Nevertheless, wherever there is causal *explanation*, there is some generalisation, implicit or explicit; and wherever an explanation is *causal*, it will be because one occurrence is being said to depend on another. This is a shorthand way of putting it, since 'occurrences' are the outcome of operations of their participants, and it is the operations and not the occurrences which are causes. Generalisation, dependence, operation, are needed for causal explanations. There can be wider and narrower generalisations; also more than one form of dependence and of operation. The notion of 'cause' is neither a single nor a simple one, and it is time to look further into its complexity.

7 Multiple Causes and the Multiplicity in 'Cause'

Factors are often selected as causes in a state of affairs by reference to some particular interest, or some practical possibility of manipulation. I have taken examples mainly from contexts where it might be hoped that the diagnosis of causes would suggest policies for controlling, eradicating, or encouraging them, as the case might be. This attempt to isolate a cause can therefore have its uses, but it can also have its dangers, when a unique cause is looked for in a situation where there are multiple interacting factors, and where concentration on altering one of them without attention to these may not produce the desired result, or may have unintended consequences in its repercussions. (The monetarist diagnosis of the cause of inflation and its cure through control of the money supply may be an instance). Still more can we be suspicious of grand over-all single causes as explaining social phenomena; for instance, Marxist explanations of social, including cultural, changes as functions of the organisation of the means of production, or Montesquieu's attributing differences in political 'climate' to differences in actual geographical climate. (It is pleasing to think that the English are not prone to tyranny because their climate is so horrible that it makes them politically active. They are too uncomfortable to sit back and relax.)[1]

Moreover, single cause views can fail to take account of how tendencies may be mutually reinforcing. An instance is Weber's view of Calvinism as the cause of capitalism.[2] Weber (and following him, R. H. Tawney[3]) said that the Calvinist godly selfdiscipline in thrift and hard work caused Puritan businessmen to save and use their savings to make money. Marxists have countered by saying that the motivation to make money was disguised as a godly self-discipline. Yet religion and the desire for business success are both strong motivations, and if they come together, between them they can produce a forceful type of character, which in this case became dominant in a suitable technological environment. To look for networks of factors rather than strands of hard-line linear causation is even more appropriate in historical than in sociological explanations, since in history the element of generalisation is recessive (though not entirely absent) and what is dominant is the presentation of complex happenings in which human participants interact with their natural and institutional environments. Thus, though history is the sphere in which the notion of 'event' is most at home, the model of event causation (*A*-like events regularly followed by *B*-like events under a covering law) fits the historical less than it does the natural world. This is partly because of the difficulty of seeing just how the historical event is bounded. The wider the complex of happenings covered by what is called the 'event', the more difficult it is to assign *a* cause, and the less possible to see it as an instance of a generalisation.

There was a Roman historian known as 'Malaria Jones', who held that the decline and fall of the Roman Empire was due to debilitation of the population through malaria. Clearly, if 'the decline and fall of the Roman Empire' is an event, it is one of very great complexity, and is a piece of shorthand for a large number of happenings, which could include environmental changes and the activities of large numbers of people. If the event as a whole is to be explained on the model of event causation, there would need to be a general law, for example to the effect that empires whose population gets debilitated through disease will collapse. This could be plausible; such a suggested cause may well draw attention to a contributory factor of importance hitherto overlooked. But note that there are rival suggestions, including Gibbon's 'the triumph of barbarism and religion'. This is in fact a general characterisation, linking a very large number of different events. These are events which might or might not have happened in the way they did. They are not like standing conditions in conjunction with which the hypothesis of the cause of the decline and fall could be deduced. So historical explanations show interconnections between numbers of particular events, including the actions and presumed motives of human participants. This does not, however, mean, as has sometimes been asserted, that historical events are unique in the sense that no generalisations come in. There is a distinction between the kind of generalisation which is a law of which the particular historical event would be an instance, and tacit generalisations about human motivations, about deprivations producing misery, and about disaffection leading to violence. Such latter generalisations are assumed in making a likely narrative. Sometimes the account may point to a generalisation of a more law-like kind, such as de

Tocqueville's, that revolutions are more likely to occur when oppressed classes are beginning to come up rather than when they are at the bottom of their deprivation. This could be supported by the presumption that if people were hungry and desolate beyond a point, they would not have the energy to organise a revolution. So causal explanation even in history draws on generalisations – otherwise there could not even be an interconnected and likely story. Occasionally the narrative may point to a non-obvious generalisation such as de Tocqueville's – the sort of generalisation which is the sociologist's dream. More often it draws on tacit commonsensical observations about how human beings are likely to behave in certain kinds of circumstances under the pressures of certain kinds of natural environment. These are generalisations about what is probable, and they may not apply in a particular case. Some historical narrative is a matter of showing how something was possible, not how it was probable, still less inevitable. This has been well put by W. H. Dray, whose *Laws and Explanations in History*[4] is the best account of the use of generalisation in historical explanation I know.

To return to 'single cause' views: These can uncover an important factor hitherto unrecognised. They can however, be dangerous where the attractive simplification they offer becomes the basis of an ideology. Seeing the world in terms of causes of a single kind may also go with seeing their instances in isolable linear chains (what I call 'hard-line causation'). This may be due to a defensible dislike of the (generally idealist) view that everything is related to everything else, so that every cause becomes in the end the whole state of the universe, which explains nothing. But this need not be the alternative. We can indeed look for causal chains, but remember that they will be subject to standing conditions and variable conditions, so that they operate *ceteris paribus* within networks, where there are multiple influences, and where multiple effects may fan out in all directions. On 30 April 1927 the *New Statesman* and other weekly journals carried a long advertisement for a post at the Malting House School, Cambridge, for a scientist 'to investigate and conduct the introduction of young children $4\frac{1}{2}$–10 to science and scientific method', and to look at the question of 'the apprehension of multiple and permissive causality which is painful to the human mind with its innate tendency to accept and manufacture explanations in terms of unitary and magical causality'. We are not told what 'permissive causality' is. Contingent? (This was of course before Piaget's work on the development of the child's conception of causality.)

To stress multiple causation is not only to put a philosophical position; to neglect it can have dangerous practical effects in social contexts, and also deleterious intellectual effects in scientific arguments, limiting the lines on which people are prepared to investigate.

This is brought out by Patrick Bateson in a paper 'Genes, Development and Learning'.[5] He speaks of the variety of conditions which can affect the development of a behaviour pattern, illustrating this from experiments on the pecking of day-old chicks and on filial imprinting whereby the young become attached to a particular member of their species. (Or, as Lorenz showed, sometimes to a member of another species, even of *Homo Sapiens*). These conditions are both internal and external; they may operate to initiate qualitatively distinct forms of behaviour, to facilitate processes already in operation, or predispose the animal to behave in a particular way without acting as a trigger. He contrasts recognition of the complexity of interacting influences with the propensity of some research workers (he has certain kinds of geneticist particularly in mind) to talk in terms of one kind of cause, and to suppose that a factor detected by their experimental manipulation will be '*the* cause'. 'Other factors which might also have an effect are ignored or, worse still, are regarded as irrelevant.' Of course to select a factor which can be produced or prevented by our manipulation is one way of naming a cause. But this can be highly misleading if taken as giving a sufficient explanation of a complex process; it can blinker one from looking at how a variety of influences can interact, or how a behavioural goal may be reached in more than one way.

So we may look for causes as selected factors; but the factor selected may vary as to how it relates to others in different contexts and in some contexts it may not be the relevant one to consider.[6] Moreover, to concentrate on linear chains of cause and effect will lead to ignoring the multiple contributing factors on the causal side, and the multiple repercussions on the effect side.

Zeno Vendler recognises concrete complexity on the side of effects, but not on the side of causes, and therefore recommends a divorce in the customary marriage of cause and effect. He holds that causes are facts, which are proposition-like, whereas effects are actual changes and processes in the world. So he suggests that 'causes' should be paired with 'results' or 'consequences', which, like causes, can be limited, and expressed in propositional form; they can be mentioned, believed, or disbelieved, whereas effects can be violent, or unexpected, or go on indefinitely.[7]

I am not convinced by this asymmetry. I am sure that Vendler is right in being worried about the abstractness of causes, when presented in proposition-like phrases such as 'that the ship struck an iceberg'.

Vendler favours a 'verb-nominalisation' (a verb-like phrase used like a noun) for effects: 'the sinking of the ship'. The cause could also be given as a nominalisation: 'the striking of an iceberg caused the sinking of the ship'. He claims 'The striking of an iceberg' can be turned into a fact clause, whereas the effect cannot, though a result clause might be. Certainly it would be clumsy to say 'that the ship struck an iceberg was the cause that the ship sank', while one might say 'had the result that the ship sank'. There may be more to this than a mere grammatical idiom.

Be this as it may, my present concern is with the supposed distinction of kind between cause and effect. Zeno Vendler wants us to accept the recommendation to reserve the word 'effects' for concrete processes, and to call the nominalisations which are paired with causes 'results'. But in practice, people will go on marrying cause and effect. More to the point philosophically, with regard to the distinction of kind, a cause as single factor described in a noun-phrase can be contrasted with all the actual influences playing on an actual situation, and similarly an effect as a single linear result can be contrasted with all the spreading repercussions. Why should we have

where the dotted line indicates that the cause is proposition-like, and the firm lines that the effects are actual happenings? Why should we not have

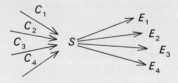

where there are a number of actual causal factors playing on a situation (S) producing a number of actual effects? In this case, a number of happenings can verge on a core situation, and a number of other happenings fan out from it. Since I hold that it is not events themselves, but the operations of their participants, which are causes, I should have to say that this is elliptical. We do indeed nominalise an event and say, e.g. 'my car breaking down caused my being late'. But 'my car breaking down' is a shorthand expression which can only be used in a causal statement because of a mechanical fault of some part of the car, so that something failed to work. I should, however, be prepared to speak of events *tout court* as effects, and in this way have an asymmetry between causes and effects though not the same as Vendler's.

Causes and effects are alike in being multiple, and this makes them more difficult to diagnose. Even if we were prepared to say with Mill that 'the real cause is all the antecedents' this would be of no use to us. If we are to use 'cause' at all, either as an explanatory or as a practical notion, it will be as a factor which can be selected from others. We might still say that all these factors are playing on the situation (as in the second figure) whether we know it or not. But if the notion of cause is to be of any service, it must be used of a select factor or factors. Just to say that it is all very complicated and all sorts of factors come in, though true, is not helpful. It can be a way of squashing people who are trying to isolate a factor and trace its effects, especially when it is a question of doing something about them. We have to select, and we have to treat factors as isolable, both in the interests of practice and in looking for explanations. An explanation is never total; it never gets in everything relevant.[8] A causal explanation is an attempt to answer a particular question about 'Why did/does x happen?' or 'Why is x like this?' by reference to something done by something else. This need not be a matter of a change in x, though it usually is. There may be a causal account of persistence or stability in x.

I have said that a number of factors can have contributed to x happening or being as it is, and the question of cause will be asked in a context where certain aspects of x are those with which we are concerned. So the appropriateness of an explanatory answer may be geared to the kind of interest that prompts the question. Of course where an interest dictates the material content of the answer we have bias; this is not the same as an interest dictating the kind of answer we are looking for. So a causal explanation in a legal case will be directed towards some abnormality in a situation; in a breakdown in a car it can be directed to finding a mechanical fault; in a disease, to isolating a particular germ. The last example shows how single-type causes have their limits. You do not always get a disease when you meet a germ; the immunological state of the body is relevant, and so sometimes are states of mind, as the success of some kinds of alternative medicine can show. In the case of the mechanical fault in an artifact, there may be counteracting devices built in, such as a cut-out, to shut off some of the effects the fault would otherwise have. In the case of an organism, countervailing processes may come into play.

Besides looking for causes in the functionings, and breakdowns of functioning, in mechanical systems and in organisms, we can look for them in the happenings of social life. Societies, whatever quasi-metaphysical theorists may have said, are neither organisms nor mechanisms. They are networks of human activities within a physical environment, some of which are channelled into institutional forms, some of which are sporadic and individual. Some of these activities are deliberate, others habitual; both kinds have repercussions in unintended consequences. Here is a natural field for the view of a cause as a happening or a property which makes *more likely* some other happening or some other property in the same thing or in something else. A likelihood, can be increased by various factors, so that no one of them need be a unique cause; different factors can be the proper object of attention in different contexts. I do not accept the view of Professor Winch and others[9] that social processes are exclusively to be explained by people's reasons, a reason being that there is a rule which they believe they should follow, and that reasons are not causes. On the kind of view I have given of a cause as a factor given in explanation of why something happened or happens, having a reason can be a cause. 'Reasons' as cited in social explanations are likely to be presented as beliefs and desires providing motives. Motives can have a causal role, but this need not lead to determinism; they can, as is said, incline without necessitating, and one may decide whether or not to act on a reason. In any case, the correlation of cause and effect is generally probabilistic, and the correlation may vary with circumstances.

An instance is current discussion of the value of giving longer sentences than normal on protectionist grounds to people who have committed violent crimes. This can be argued largely, if not exclusively, on the reliability of predicting the deterrent effect of the sentences on the likelihood of these people committing further violent crimes. Professor Nigel Walker writes:

There are certainly plausible reasons for supposing that a reputation for dishonesty will often make subsequent dishonesty more likely. It makes it harder to get a legitimate job. People who keep their social distance from a known thief make him more likely to associate with other thieves in a similar position . . . Slightly less plausible is the assertion that his 'self image' may be so damaged by the label that, thinking of himself as a thief, he will have less resistance to temptation to steal. This is more plausible when the label is regarded as a diagnosis: for example, the label 'drug addict' or 'alcoholic'. Even so, such a label may arouse enough anxiety to induce the subject to demonstrate that he does not merit it, and may thus have a beneficial influence.[10]

The last sentence shows that social activities often have feedbacks; what is an effect at one stage of an on-going process can have a causal influence on a supervening stage, either to correct it, or (in the case of negative feedback) to reinforce it. Moreover, this kind of discussion shows that if we say that a person has a disposition to commit a certain kind of crime, it is not enough to say this is a way of predicting the probability that he will commit such crimes in the future. A disposition is not only a set of hypothetical propositions; the probability can be increased or diminished by known information about his actual character, and this is no doubt taken into account by those who have to consider long sentences for protective reasons. But they will know well that their predictions of the likelihood of future violent conduct fall short of certainty; and this, sometimes tragically, is also the case where the *unlikelihood* of future violent conduct is predicted.

In his book *Behaviour and Misbehaviour: explanations and non-explanations*[11] Professor Walker looks at multiple-factor views of the causes of crime, as contrasted with those views which seek to link all the variables in a single theory applicable to all cases. He defends a multiple-factor view against the charge of being merely eclectic by saying that if the number of factors suggested is finite, and each can be tested in the relevant circumstances, this can be a serious scientific approach to the diagnosis of causes. A 'multiple factor view' can mean that in any given case there are a number of contributory factors; this would hardly be open to dispute. He is concerned rather to use this expression to mean that there are different kinds of causes of crime, which cannot all be shown to follow from one overall cause. He deals faithfully with the theory of the authors of *The New Criminology* (a significant title)[12] who say that the cause of crime is the Criminal Law. This is an example of a 'formal cause'; if there were no Criminal Law, nothing indeed would be *called* a crime. But this gives no explanation for why the Criminal Law should fasten on certain kinds of behaviour, and why measures are taken to deter them. If we say that but for the Criminal Law people would not, for example, break into each other's houses (or if they did, nothing would have to be done about it), this is a veiled recommendation for anarchism. (Of course to say no one should be charged with a crime unless he is believed to have committed an act which is a crime by law is an important principle of natural justice, but that is a different matter from a view of the cause of crime.) An example of a substantive view of an overall cause of crime would be a Freudian theory. Walker cites the late Edward Glover, who said that 'the unconscious need for punishment' was 'the key to all problems of delinquency'.[13] My cousin John Watson, who was a juvenile court magistrate, quotes an explanation of the cause of a piece of delinquency more convincing than that suggested by another piece of Freudian theory:

> Bobby Short stole a wedding dress. It was encased in an enormous cardboard box, by far the largest of the parcels in the couturier's van which its driver had carelessly left at the curb with the doors open. The fact that a boy of twelve had stolen a wedding dress had all the Freudian disciples on tiptoe. But the woman chairman of the court thought she would put a few questions before deciding whether a psychiatric examination was called for. Why, she asked him, had he stolen the largest box in the van which must have been very difficult to get away with? 'Yer see, Miss,' he answered confidently, 'I wer wanting a box for my puss-cat to do 'er business in; and my puss-cat's a very *big* puss-cat.'[14]

The trouble with over-all theories is that they may foreclose the search for simpler possible causal explanations.

Walker quotes[15] Durkheim's maxim '*à un même effet correspond toujours une même cause*', and says that as a statement of fact, a particular effect, for example a car being overturned in a ditch, may have been due to various causes. He thinks Durkheim intended the remark as a methodological principle (it appears in the *Rules of Sociological Method*): where there are different kinds of causes, look for different kinds of effect, and vice versa. Durkheim's own example was that of kinds of suicide. I think, however, that it is not straightforward to say that this lets us correlate different kinds of causes with different kinds of effects. There may be different kinds of suicide: for example suicides where a person wants to draw attention to himself, and suicides where he wants to end unbearable pain. The end effect, say death from an overdose of a drug, could be the same; the classification into different kinds builds the causal motive into the definition of the kind. To say that the cause of a suicide of the type which consists of drawing attention to oneself will be the desire to draw attention to oneself will be tautological except for the word 'desire'. One must allow that the same effect – death from an overdose of a drug – could be led up to by different causes, and try and see which may have been operating in this case. A simple 'same effect, same cause' view in cases of social phenomena (as suicide) comes up against the fact that social causation has to include motives as well as physical events. As a physical event, one might say the cause of the death was the swallowing of a drug of a certain chemical composition. As a social event, one might look for a cause further back in the suicide's state of mind. Durkheim, of course, would not allow that states of mind were relevant to social causation, which may be one reason why he recommends the simple rule of 'same cause, same effect'. I doubt whether many sociologists would follow him in his exclusion of psychological states of mind – which is not to say that sociology with its proper interest in the institutional structure of situations and in unintended consequences, can just be identified with social psychology.

The more pertinent objection to Durkheim's maxim, for my present concern, is that it commits us to what I have called 'hard-line causation', single, isolated chains of cause and effect, instead of allowing for multiple causes in the sense of networks of interrelated factors, or for the possibility of different routes leading up to the same end result. The end result might be the derailment of a train, and the immediate cause might be its striking an obstacle on the line. The explanation of how the obstacle got there might be that it was a fall of rock; or it might be a rock placed as an act of vandalism for a dare; or it might have been placed as an act of political terrorism; or as an act of protest against the train's transporting nuclear waste. The immediate cause was the train's striking the obstacle; the interest for social explanation is in something further back: how did the obstacle get there, and if it was placed, what were the motives of the people who placed it?

So the notion of a cause is neither a single nor a simple one. It is not a single one, because of what Mill called 'the plurality of causes'. Mill meant by this that the same effect may follow on different causes – death from poisoning or death from drowning. More to the point, the 'plurality of causes' may mean a plurality of causal influences, no one of which by itself being sufficient, though there may be good reasons for fastening attention on one rather than another in a particular context. The cause need not be single; but nor is the notion of cause simple, in the sense that there is just one type of cause. There may be different kinds of principle which can be brought into what are called causal explanations. The 'plurality of causes' may not only mean a number of causal factors of the same type, but also a plurality of types of cause.

Aristotle saw this complexity, and it led him to make distinctions, the chief of which are in what we know as his doctrine of the Four Causes.[16] Of these, only the Efficient, and, in intentional contexts, the Final Cause look like causes in the sense in which we normally use the word. We should not normally speak of the material out of which something comes as a cause, nor of the 'Formal Cause', the principle defining what it is to be something of that kind, as a cause. Aristotle, however, is connecting 'cause' with explanation of why something is as it is, and listing the kinds of factor which have a role in this.[17]

For Aristotle, things (other than God and pure intelligences, if such there be) are what they are because there is matter (in a very general sense) out of which they are produced, and there is form in the matter for them to be things of a particular kind. There is also the action of something or somebody in shaping the matter, and the end for which it is shaped. Of these four, the efficient cause is a principle of change, and can originate change: where change carries out a purpose, the latter is the final cause. When there is no attribution of conscious purpose, the formal and final causes coalesce; a thing develops through its power to achieve the form of a thing of that species. Form, as intelligible structure, is to be taken into account in explaining why something is as it is; and so too are its material, its efficient, and its final causes.

Aristotle's word for 'cause' was $\alpha\dot{\imath}\tau\dot{\imath}\alpha$; to say someone or something was $\alpha\dot{\imath}\tau\iota o\nu$ was ordinarily to say he or it was accountable for something. Aristotle has, I think, shed, or almost shed, the anthropomorphic overtones, especially where $\alpha\dot{\imath}\tau\dot{\imath}\alpha$ suggests blame, just as he has shed the overtones of 'ruling' in the word $\alpha\rho\chi\dot{\eta}$ used in the sense which we translate as 'principle'. $\alpha\rho\chi\dot{\eta}$ still, has the overtone of priority, but priority either as being a premise in deduction or as being an explanatory factor.

Aristotle's causes are thus 'becauses', all of which can come in when we try to give a complete account of why something is as it is. In general, he defines a cause as the origin of a change in something or of something staying unchanged.[18] Note that something remaining unchanged requires causal explanation as well as its change. (I shall be looking later at views which say this). Moreover, he sees omissions as well as commissions as possible causes: 'That which, by being present, is the cause of so and so, is sometimes held responsible ($\alpha\dot{\imath}\tau\iota o\nu$) by its absence for the opposite; thus the loss of a ship is set down to the absence of the steersman, whose presence would have been the cause of its being saved.'[19] This constructs a counterfactual – if the steersman had been present, the ship would have been saved. (On the reasonable assumption that it could not have been lost for another cause, the steersman, by being absent, is held responsible). Aristotle, then, has a plurality of causes not only as a multiplicity of efficient causal influences (though these need not be excluded), but as different kinds of principle to be taken into account in explaining why *A* is as it is or happens as it does. The complexity is in the kinds of cause.[20]

Nevertheless, it might be said that he still gears his account of causation to what needs to be taken into account in explaining the result of something done by some agency. In his example of the statue, this is produced by the chisel blows of the sculptor on the material of the marble, shaping it to a form which will finally be the figure whose portrait the sculptor intends to sculpt. Fine, so long as we are talking about the different kinds of factor to be taken into account where an agent deliberately produces something. Aristotle, did, as I have said, try to de-anthropomorphise this account by coalescing the formal and final causes in describing natural processes. Even so, is his account plausible except where there is an association with the idea of human agency?

I shall have more to say about this in Chapter 10, in looking at causation in organisms. Here I have been concerned to note that Aristotle's distinction of kinds of cause suggests efficient causation – the action of one thing on another *ab extra* – is not the only kind. This has been called 'transeunt causation', and it is the usual view. There may be other and more internal ways in which one thing depends on another. If these can be called 'causal', they might be described as kinds of 'immanent causation'.

8 Immanent and Transeunt Causation

'Immanent Causation' was used for agent causation by Roderick Chisholm,[1] saying that he was reviving a mediaeval distinction. The mediaevals claimed to derive this distinction from Aristotle's *Metaphysics*:[2]

> When the result is something apart from the exercise [of producing it], the actualizing is in the thing that is being made, e.g., the act of building is in the thing that is being built . . . but when there is no product apart from the actualizing [in the producing], the actualizing is in the agent, e.g., the seeing is in the seeing subject and theorizing in the theorizing subject, and the life is in the soul.

St Thomas takes this over as a distinction between '*facere*' and '*agere*'. '*Factio est actus transiens in exteriorem materiam, sicut aedificare, secare et huiusmodi. Agere autem est actus permanens in ipso agente, sicut videre, velle et huiusmodi.*'[3] The distinction is between the kind of doing which transfers an activity onto something external (making), and action where the activity and its effect remain within the agent (doing). In the former case, but not the latter, the product is separable from the activity.

Chisholm mentions this distinction, calling the *actus permanens* 'immanent'. He says he may not be making the distinction in just the mediaeval way. His own distinction is between 'doing' and 'making happen'. Whenever a man does something A, then (by immanent causation) he makes a certain cerebral event happen, and this cerebral event (by 'transeunt causation') makes A happen.[4] 'Making happen' is a matter of event causation, and the agent can be unaware of some of the events. 'Doing' does not call for a further event as its cause; as an agent, one just does the action, and the action may make happen a string of events, such as the brain events, so as to make happen the thing A (for example, turning on the light) which one had undertaken. So 'doing' is

76

just something which the agent himself does and is not caused by any ulterior event (one recalls Danto's 'basic actions'). Chisholm says in acting one might say the agent is a 'prime mover' – another Aristotelian term (used here for a first efficient and not, as with Aristotle, a final cause). This is a fairly extreme view of freedom and responsibility, and runs counter to attempts to give a causal account of actions in terms of beliefs and desires. Von Wright says that he does not see that the notion of 'immanent causation' adds anything here to that of action.[5] But Chisholm is not, like von Wright, putting the action outside causation. He is distinguishing between what he calls 'doing' and 'making happen', as causal in different ways: in 'doing' what is done is internal to the act of doing it, as distinct from 'making happen', where the thing done is something external to the act. Willing can produce an external product, which it makes happen. What is not an external product is the willing itself; external, that is, to the activity in which it finds its expression.

The notion of 'immanent causation' has, however, been used more widely. 'Immanent causality' was distinguished from 'transeunt causality' by W. E. Johnson,[6] along with a distinction, between 'continuants' and 'occurrents'. This latter answers to the traditional distinction between substances and events. The 'continuant', however, need not carry the metaphysical implications which sometimes were seen in 'substance', as being a substratum distinct from its qualities. A continuant need only show a persistent character recognisable over time. 'Occurrents' are changes in a continuant, for example this particle as moving from A to B at time t. Causation for Johnson calls both for continuants and for occurrents. When one continuant is seen as external to another and acting on it, this is transeunt causation. When there is change of state within a single continuant, this is immanent causation.[7] Changes within a system taken as a whole are cases of immanent causation. But a system may be seen as composed of parts which are sub-continuants, and where changes in the system can be explained as due to the action of these on each other, they can be seen as cases of transeunt causation. So changes in the temperature, pressure and volume of a gas can be described by a law correlating their alterable states in a formula (immanent causation), or as due to the action on each other of the molecules composing the gas (transeunt causation). Changes in the molecules themselves as continuants could be described as immanent causation, unless they could be explained by the actions of sub-continuants – for example atoms. It looks as though each level of immanent causation in a system might be broken down into a further level of transeunt causation – unless there is a level at which it is impossible to go beyond changes of state in the system itself. Perhaps this is the case with the fundamental particles in quantum mechanics.

To come back to the example of the gas, where there is a systematic relation (Boyle's Law) between changes in temperature, volume and pressure (these equations hold under all conditions except those of very low temperature and very high pressure, and these conditions can be exactly specified). This could allow Johnson's immanent causation as change within a system. It does not, however, as I have said, dispense with transeunt causation where there is explanation of changes in the system in terms of the actions on each other of its sub-continuants. Thus immanent and transeunt causation are here complementary. The former is concerned with changes in a system as a whole. These can be set going by transeunt causation, where external action on the system produces a rise in temperature for example. Where 'immanent causation' is used of change within a system as a whole, this can be shown in co-temporal correlations of variables. These are co-temporal, and not successive, though one variable can be the dependent and the other the independent one. The latter is the initiating change, for example when decreasing the volume of the gas increases the pressure. Such co-temporal co-variance in a system was said by Russell to have supplanted the notion of Cause, at any rate in physics. I am prepared still to speak of causation as bringing out that one change is dependent on the other; there is not just functional co-variance. Which variable is the independent one can be due to transeunt causation by something acting on the system from outside, or the changing of a system in one way may induce changes in it in other ways. Thus immanent and transeunt causation both come into the account of change in a system seen as a continuant.

There is another sense in which causation is used of continuants. Johnson saw the identity of a continuant in a causal unity of connection between its temporarily or spatially separated manifestations. The character of the continuant at one time depends functionally, in its identity and changes, on its character at an earlier time.[8] This could be immanent causation in that changes from stage to stage are changes within the system as a continuant. Of course the properties may not change, except in so far as there is the change from being the system at one stage to being that system at another stage. If this is immanent causation, it is a different kind from co-temporal co-variable change in a system. The dependence is that of one temporal stage on the preceding one.

It might be tempting to say that transition from stage to stage is transeunt if anything is. It might be so if all that need be said is that an earlier stage is the cause of the later stage as effect. I want to say more than this: the system persists as a continuant. I started from the distinction between causation where there is a product apart from the activity of producing and where the product is internal to the producing. In persistence in a continuant seen as a matter of immanent causation, the stages are not separate elements, but are distinguished as stages in a single on-going process. This adds the notion of process to that of mere continuance. The continuant is persisting through maintaining its stability.

Maintenance of stability is of course more than just persistence; it depends on processes coming into play in resistence to external forces and it is natural to try to describe these causally. Where the fact of persistence itself is seen as causal, it is necessary to have either a very strong or a weak view of causation. It could accord with a weak view if all causation need mean is that something is more likely to have a certain property at one stage if it had had a certain property at an earlier stage. D. H. Mellor says this, (notably he does not think that it is all that need be meant by causation but it is sufficient for the purpose of his book), and he invokes causation for an unchanging thing having properties at a later time as being more likely because it has had them earlier.

A thing's having a property at any time is causally explained by its having had it earlier, given that the thing was not then in another state entailing or probabilifying change in this respect, and no change has occurred in it meanwhile . . . The only cause of a stage of an unchanging thing is an immediately preceding and otherwise identical stage of the same thing, whose only effect is its otherwise undistinguished successor.[9]

Mackie, in *The Cement of the Universe*, also extends causation to apply to persistence. His earlier view of cause as a INUS condition (a condition which is insufficient but necessary in a complex of conditions which are unnecessary but sufficient), was, of course, a 'selected factor view', where the factor selected was a *conditio sine qua non*. He now calls this 'neolithic causation'.[10] It has its uses, but the more subtle underlying concept is that of qualitative or structural continuity in processes, which, he says, may stem from basic laws of working, so that what happens next '*flows from*' what is there already; 'the immediate present is, so to speak, *extruded* by the present and the immediate past'.[11] He sums this up in a picturesque phrase 'the universe needs to know where to go next'. 'Flows from' and 'extruded' are strong words, suggesting not only an epistemology but a metaphysics. Mackie did not, however, develop these metaphors into what might have been a strong view of causation.

A strong view would be a metaphysical one. This could involve holding that an account needs to be given of persistence which connects it with other basic concepts used in a view of the world, of which one is notably causation. It would not be sufficient just to say that P continuing or persisting over time is implied in calling P a continuant. Nor is to say that P persists just to say that P at one time is the same thing as P at another (accepting that some of its properties may have changed). Indeed it is prior to the question of identity, since if P did not persist, the question of identity, of whether P at time$_1$ is the same as P at time$_2$, would not arise. Persistence is, of course, more than just continuity. There can be continuity, for instance, in a series of events where each has a common boundary with the next; the events succeed each other continuously, but do not persist. Persistence goes with identity; P at one time is still P at another time. So there needs to be something which persists (in Johnson's continuant, this was a character at one time as functionally dependent on a character at another time).

David Wiggins in *Sameness and Substance*[12] has brought out the distinction between continuity and identity. He also distinguishes between identity as a primitive concept (this P at time$_1$ is the same as that P at time$_2$) and the *criteria* of identity – how do we tell that one thing is the same as another? These are connected, in that for P at one time to be the same as P at another time, it must be something of the same kind. There must be a predicate (called in the literature a 'sortal' predicate), which specifies something as a member of a particular kind, for example a horse; we can then ask 'Is this the same horse as I saw yesterday?' There will need also to be a path through space and time which this horse I see today has followed if it was the horse I saw yesterday – otherwise the sortal predicate would only give an answer to the question 'Is this animal I am now seeing a horse?'. Wiggins' view, I believe, bears most closely on my present concerns where he asks what predicates are most profitably used as sortal predicates for 'natural' kinds. He says they will not be those describing obvious apparent characteristics (one recalls the old definition of man as a featherless biped), but those that connect an agreed (paradigm) example of the class, for example a horse, with a law-like principle which will show the constitution of something of that kind at a deep level. Also, in the case of living things, this will need to be a principle allowing their development from one life stage to another, and, on an evolutionary development, allow (as Aristotle did not) for phylogenetic development. To find principles of this kind for classifying species is of course, the deep problem in taxonomy.[13] Such principles would show how 'to be something of that kind is to exemplify the distinctive mode of activity that they determine'.[14] This remark is highly congenial to a view which I should like to hold of immanent causation as a mode of functioning internal to a system, and producing change and development over time. I have not yet been so bold as to call this a mode of '*activity*'. Wiggins does call it this; he does not elaborate on the word 'activity'; however, he says that the principles selected as 'sortal', if they are to be profitable, should be ones through which some headway can be made over explanation and causality.

I have so far used the word 'functioning' where Wiggins has said a 'mode of activity'. He reserves 'function' as a condition for the identity of *artifacts* as distinct from natural kinds. The sortal concept for an artifact would be the function for which it was designed; as in Aristotle's example of a house as a shelter against destruction by wind, rain and heat. In the case of artifacts, there might well have to be a stipulative decision as to whether, for example, a certain shelter was a house; here planning and rating officers have to decide whether a certain shelter counts as a house in the sense of a 'residence'. Also, there is the question, which Wiggins discusses, of how far preservation of function through displacement of parts and substitution of others allows one to call an artifact the same. The classical example was Theseus' ship, where new planks had been substituted for all the old planks.[15] Was it the same ship? Here Wiggins is inclined to say it was, if there were overlaps in the substitution of new for old planks before the whole ship had been renewed.

I should be inclined to say that in the case of artifacts there is a stronger element of stipulation than in the case of living things. There is no principle of internal development of a ship from stage to stage, though there are principles on which it is constructed. The parts have been put together to serve an external purpose of the designer, and this is their 'function'. (*Pace* Aristotle, we do not think of living things and human beings as having a 'function' in this sense, though there is indeed a sense in which we speak of them as functioning through the internal relations of their parts, and I shall more to say about this later.) So an artifact is a system of parts constructed to serve a function, and the parts are replaceable. It is therefore appropriate to see the interaction of the parts in the system, and the use of the whole artifact to effect the purpose for which it was designed, as showing transeunt causation. We can define it as the same artifact either by reference to its function or the materials of which it is composed, if these have not all been changed at once. I have said there is an element of stipulation here. I use my shoe for hammering in nails; this is an acquired function not intended by the shoemaker.[16]

Identity through change of parts can be defended by saying the parts are put together and can be taken apart, and so are substitutable without destroying the system. In the case of living things, there can, we know, be some substitutions, for example plastic hips and organ transplants. But there is also the problem of rejection of the transplant. The system has its internal adjustments. So, it may be said, have some artifacts, for example the thermostat on a boiler, where regulators have been built into the design of the artifact. But the homeostatic adjustments in the organism develop internally, and there are a great many of them which can come into play together.

In the case of artifacts, there may be known principles of the *modus operandi* of the parts which explain this through transeunt causation. In the case of living things, sometimes transeunt causation can be shown in homeostatic chemical reactions within the system, which, barring blockages and countervailing attacks, will bring it back into equilibrium. There is still the process of the development of the system, which, I think, needs to be described by immanent causation. I shall be saying more about this in Chapter 10: it is a well-known problem of the philosophy of biology. I return here to the overtly metaphysical problem not of development, but of mere persistence. Does the persistence of anything in any shape or form whatever need a strong view of causation?

A philosopher who thought that it did was A. N. Whitehead. He was impressed by the thought that persistence cannot be taken for granted, and he connected it with a strong metaphysics of 'Causal Efficacy'. Whitehead's views, especially in his later works, where this became explicit, are fraught with complexities. This is so above all in *Process and Reality*, where they are couched in a psycho-physiological language of 'feelings'. I shall not embark on an exposition of these later views, the language of which I should not want to defend, but try to go behind them to see why he thinks that the persistence of processes, in what he calls 'the passage of nature', is a matter of causal *efficacy*.

Whitehead, more perhaps than any other philosopher, saw a metaphysical problem in how there could be a 'becoming of continuity', rather than a 'continuity of becoming'.[17] He has told us that throughout his life he was preoccupied by the question of how the past continually perishes and yet is perpetuated (how?) in the present. In some reflections on *Process and Reality* given at Harvard in 1932[18] he said: 'If you get a general notion of what is meant by perishing, you will have accomplished an apprehension of what you mean by memory and causality.' He said he had been concerned to analyse 'perishing' as Aristotle analysed 'becoming' – how what is past perishes, and yet is an element in a state beyond itself (presumably, analogously to the way in which for Aristotle the future is not yet, but is an element – *qua* potentiality – in a present state). Our basic sense of the world is, he said, of something going on, what he called 'the passage of nature'. What passes is gone: as Heraclitus said, you cannot step twice into the same river. Yet we recognise recurrent patterns and properties in the passage – otherwise there would be no articulated perceptions.

In his earlier books Whitehead put the distinction between what passes and what can be recurrently recognised in terms of the distinction between 'events' and 'objects'. I have already referred to his view of 'events' as slices of the passage of nature; 'objects' are adjectives qualifying events, which can 'be again'. An object, he says,[19] is 'an ingredient in the character of some event'. Objects answer to what more generally would be called properties as universals. Any event of which we can be aware – for example, the event called the clock striking twelve – must be qualified by objects. Events could not be bounded apart from 'objects' – nor could there be any awareness of them unless they were characterised. Objects on their own are pure potentials. There is, of course, the Platonic view which gives them a kind of actual existence, and Whitehead has been taken as Platonist, especially in the later books where he speaks of 'eternal objects'. I did this myself in an early work;[20] I refer to this book (which is now properly superseded) only for the reason that it drew a personal rejoinder from Whitehead in one of his rare letters; what he says bears directly on the question of persistence in the passage of nature and also on the repetition of characters in it in terms of causal efficacy, and as it is this with which I am concerned, I will quote the letter. 'At times you write as if the connection between past and present is merely that of a transfer of character. Then there arises (*sic*) all the perplexities of "correspondence" in epistemology, of causality and of memory', and he calls attention to his doctrines of 'immanence' and 'conformal feelings'.

So he repudiates a mere view of sequences of events with recognisable, because repeated, characteristics (objects) which could go with a Humean view of causation. He repudiates this because it does not go far enough back into our basic experience, which is of transition – our present experience comes to us as arising out of a past experience; it may, if you like, be that of a fraction of a second ago. Also it is directed towards a next stage, which could be that of a fraction of a second hence. This recalls William James's notion of the 'specious present', taken not only subjectively, as a feature of our experience, but as saying something about the world from which our experience arises. It is a world of transitions with spatio–temporal spread. How do we get this continuity out of a 'perpetual perishing' (Locke's expression)?

If this is seen causally, it is not the kind of causation where one factor is selected from a complex of factors in some state of affairs. We are dealing with processes, and their persistence from a vanishing past in to a yet not existing future. It is immanent causation of a kind where there is active transition from one phase to another. This may seem an unwarrantably strong view; I shall try to say more later to justify it. I see no half way between a view of this kind and that of a succession of events, none of which is allowed to change, and where there is no *changing* apart from change interpreted as a successor event having a different property or properties from its predecessor. And why then should there be a successor?

Causation is invoked to explain changes, and persistence might be said to be the simplest kind of change, from one phase of, say, a system, to another. In another sense, this could of course be called a non-change, if the properties of the system remain the same. But even that is a change from being the system as it was into being the system as it is. Where persistence is spoken of causally, this can be a weak view if all that is meant is that if something has had a certain property in the past it will probably have it in the future, especially in the very near future.

It can, however, be a strong view, as a claim that something which is passing is also carrying itself forward into its next stage. This does not only mean that later stages are likely to display the same properties as earlier ones, nor is it cause and effect in temporal succession. It means that persistence is possible because of an internal activity directed towards the future, and the product is inseparable from the activity. Spinoza spoke of a thing having a *conatus in suo esse perseverandi*, and this comes near to suggesting this on-going activity. I should not want to use the word '*esse*' as suggesting an essential nature. Nor should I want to talk about continuants as having 'intrinsic natures, shown in causal powers.'[21] This seems to me to savour of a hankering after Aristotelian real definitions, which are then made effective as formal causes; it does not allow enough for radical changes in continuants. Rather than talking about 'natures' I should prefer to think of a thing having, in Locke's phrase, a 'real internal constitution', maintained dynamically, partly through internal homeostatic 'feedbacks', in which an aberration at one stage may be corrected at the next; the whole thing is in movement, the pattern gets carried on from one time span of its history to the next – until of course some disturbance is too much for it. This carrying forward of a pattern, perhaps in a rhythmic reiterative form, may go both for fundamental particles, the distribution of whose activities is given in the mathematics of wave mechanics, and also for organisms, and for whatever other natural units there may be in between.

Even if we do not assume essential natures, to invoke causation to talk about persistence, including persistence of a pattern, sounds odd, since causation is normally invoked in talking about change. We normally think that it is change, and not persistence, as non-change, which needs explanation. Newton's First Law of Motion might be taken as supporting this: 'Every body continues in its state of rest, or uniform motion in a straight line, unless it is compelled by impressed forces to change that state.' What have to be explained are changes of state. Even so, inertia, the continuance of a state, whether of rest or motion, is the subject of a law. It is not just taken for granted. The law is a law of motion, of which rest is a particular case. Newton did not call his First Law of Motion a causal law. It describes a condition with no change of state; where there is change of state, he did not call force its cause; this might have savoured of 'occult causes'. Force is needed for work to be done by the communication of energy. It is said that kinetic energy need only mean the measurement of work done in motion, e.g. in the acceleration of x from A to B, and potential energy the capacity for work that would be done, if (for example) a coiled-up spring were released. But one may want also to say that the coiled-up spring stores potential energy in a categorical and not only a hypothetical dispositional sense,[22] and it is this which does the work in kinetic energy when the spring is released. Energy would then be a name for something which actually does work, and not only a name for its measurement. If it is said that energy need only mean the measurement of work, then the buck is passed to the word 'work'; if 'work' means measurable change, for example in momentum, then the buck is passed to the word 'change'. Wherever we go, from forces to energy, to work, to changes, we get to some point where we are talking of a happening which is an effect and not only talking of its measurement. I see the 'effecting' as an operation and what brings it about an operative; these are activity terms but not, I hope, animistic ones. My defence is that, without some such notion, we are left with a world in which there is no real movement (as distinct from recorded changes in position); no real becoming (as distinct from descriptions of successive states); no real persistence (as distinct from prediction of properties at later times from earlier ones). The phrases enclosed in brackets have a place in theoretical contexts; but they are abstractions from a world in which actual operations actually take effect.

So I see the world as a world of operations. Some of these are the action of one thing on another; what has been called transeunt causation. Some are activities within a system as a whole, where the product is not separable from the activity of producing it: what has been called immanent causation. Seeing the persisting existence of something as a matter of immanent causation calls for a stronger view than the likelihood of its having certain properties at a later time because it has had these or other properties at an earlier one. In any case, existence, it is generally agreed, is not a property, though for something to have properties it must be there to have them. To see persistence as a matter of immanent causation is to say that the activity which is producing a present state is carried forward into the supervening state. Moreover, the supervening stage recapitulates the pattern of the subvening stage, unless something happens externally or internally to produce a variation on this.

Nothing I have said in this chapter need preclude using the word 'cause' in a weak sense in a possible epistemology where 'cause is used as a term for predicting the probability of something occurring or having a property. On a stronger view, we pass beyond the epistemology to a metaphysics underpinning it, and in this there may be a causal relation which prediction enables us to test, but which says more than that a predicted property is probable. In this chapter I have been indicating one such metaphysical view. It would allow immanent causation where some states in a process are not only functions of other states as predictable from them, but there is a pattern of *functioning* as an integrating activity continuing over a time span. (The word 'functioning' points towards a generalised notion of organism, and I shall have more to say about this in Chapter 10.)

So I see a persistent thing not just as something in which one stage follows another with resembling properties. There is an ongoing passage of nature where activity is individualised in dynamic systems and where patterns are reiterated and new ones established. Changes in these systems can sometimes be seen in terms of transeunt causation, but transeunt causation, since it happens within the passage of nature, ultimately presupposes immanent causation.

In seeing the persistence of things in terms of immanent causation, I am still, I hope, within my general view of a cause as something on which something happening to something else depends. Here the dependence is not that of a later on an earlier stage as if the latter were a temporally separable product. That something can maintain its stability does, of course, depend on contributory factors in its environment which act on it in transeunt causation. It is not just self-producing, as would I think, be suggested by the old term *causa sui*. Yet that it should persist depends on an activity which passes from stage to stage, but is internal to the passage and not temporally prior to it. I see this absence of temporal priority of cause to effect as a general characteristic of immanent causation. Immanent causation can, however, have different forms:

1. It can be co-temporal, co-variable change within a system, where variables are distinguishable, and one can depend on another.
2. There can be growth and development within the system as a whole. (I shall be saying more about this in Chapter 10).
3. There is the mere fact of persistence as dependent on an on-going activity.
4. There may be ways in which one activity works through another, but these activities cannot be distinguished, still less measured, as co-variables. (I shall look at possible instances of this in Chapters 10 and 11.)

9 Immanent Causation in Memory

I have said that I should be getting more metaphysical as I went on, and shall now press further into seeing the carrying over from stage to stage in a continuant as a matter of immanent causation.

We can start from the metaphysics in our basic experience. This, I believe, is one of movement and of transition, the passing of one state into another. Our primitive experience is of the derivation of what is going on in the present from what was going on in the immediate past. The way we finish a sentence is connected (generally speaking) with the way we have begun it; the movement of my arm when I hit a ball carries through the movement by which I raised it. And if it is said these are actions, intentional happenings, it is also the case that when I look at the world without acting on it I see things going on, and can only make sense of the present as carrying over from the immediate past. I also only make sense of it by assuming that it will continue, at any rate into the immediate future. How we expect it to continue may sometimes be rudely shaken, and we are then thrown off course. But generally speaking the immediate future is as we expect it to be, and from present experience we can often foresee coming changes and do something to forestall them. So we depend both on short-term memory and on short-term expectation for any meaningful experience: and for more interesting experience we depend on longer-term memories and more distant expectations. Memory testifies to the derivation of experience from the past, and faulty memories are parasitic on this.

Memory is a present awareness of something with a reference to the past. It may be an event in our own past, or it may be something we have observed or learnt about somebody or something else. Habitual associative memories may be *effects* of whatever stimulates them; we can predict with deadly accuracy that A will tell us a certain story if he hears a certain remark. But deliberately recollected memories, especially when 'recollected in tranquillity', are more like appropriations of some part of our inheritance from the past for our use in the present. Coleridge brings out the difference between the merely sequential kind of experience, and the memory which is consequential, which draws on the past and integrates it with present experience and future expectation (a future here anticipated in hope, not apprehension).

> It is a maxim with me, to make Life as continuous as possible, by linking on the Present to the Past: and I believe that a large portion of the ingratitude, inconstance, frivolity, and restless self-weariness so many examples of which obtrude themselves on every man of observation and reflective habits, is attributable to the *friable*, incohesive sort of existence that characterizes the mere man of the World, a fractional Life made up of successive moments, that neither blend nor modify each other – a life that is strictly symbolized in the thread of Sand thro' the orifice of the Hour-glass, in which the sequence of Grains only *counterfeits* a continuity, and appears a *line* only because the interspaces between the Points are too small to be sensible. Without memory there can be no hope – the Present is a phantom known only by its pining, if it do not breathe the vital air of the Future: and what is the Future, but the Image of the Past projected on the mist of the Unknown, and seen with a glory round it's head.[1]

So memory is the conscious appropriation in the present of something from the past. It is not a piece of time travel back into the past; the Greeks got it right when they said that Mnemosyne was a goddess who called the past into the present, not one who cast the mind back into the past:

> 'When in the sessions of sweet silent thought
> I summon up remembrance of things past . . . '

Memory has been said to be the criterion of personal identity, to which it can be said that unless I can claim memories as mine, I cannot say that I am I because of my memories. Richard Wollheim has, however, written more deeply about how memory can be criterial of personal identity.[2] Memory links us to our past, and 'If experiential memory is criterial of personal identity, it is so just because it is also creative of personal identity'. This is so because memory does not only let us know, or think we know, we have had past experiences. It also conveys their affective tone, and this can go on influencing our present beliefs, feelings and attitudes, especially through fears and anxieties. The great achievement of psycho-analysis has been to show how these can be surmounted by reawakening the past experience in memory through bringing it into consciousness. 'Living through' what is recollected can free us from barren repetitiveness in the entail of affective tone, so that we can appropriate the experience constructively as part of our past.

Memory is not inferential. I do not infer that something in the past happened because I have a present memory: indeed (analytically) memory would not be memory if it were not of the past. This is, however, not just a question of meaning. Present memory claims to be a non-inferential source of knowledge of the past. It is, of course, highly fallible and gappy, and we tend to fill the gaps with what we imagine. (Wollheim thinks that the carrying over of affective tone, what the experience felt like from inside, is a sign, though of course not an infallible one, that we did have the experience and did not imagine or hear about it.) In this, there is only a difference of degree from what we do in present perception. That also is incomplete, and we fill out and interpret what we think we see. Neither memory nor perception is incorrigible; we claim they give us non-inferential knowledge, but we can make mistakes over it.

If memory is not inferential, neither is it simply a calling up of images of past perceptions which resemble those perceptions. At any rate, there is no actual comparison of a present with a past impression. Nor, I think, is Russell's view of 'mnemic causation' very helpful.[3] 'Mnemic causation' is a term for the fact that when we have what we take to be a memory image we usually find that it has been preceded by an event in our past to which it is referred. So if we remember x, then x probably happened. This need not involve preceding events in a continuous temporal succession, in which case we would only remember immediately preceding events. There is no need to invoke more than a mere regularity view of causation. And if this is all we need for causation, 'mnemic causation' need not depend on present physical traces. It is a weak view, tying causation to retrodiction instead of to prediction.

Those who try to link memory with causation in a stronger way than this generally do it by giving a causal account in terms of physical (neural?) traces, stored presumably in the brain, and activated by a present stimulus. This is speculative, as no one has actually observed the traces. Analogies of a telephone exchange or of a computer store are not convincing, since memories are so multifarious, and integrated in so many ways, that it is implausible to think there is a trace for every memory to be coded in the brain.[4] In any case, this omits the searcher or scanner. Nor, in my opinion, is it convincing to think of memory (recollecting memory, if not habit memory) as something purely spiritual, as Bergson does.[5]

The question, as I see it, is not whether memories are mental or physical, but the nature of *consciousness*. Consciousness is not all or nothing; it fades down into the subconscious (this is common knowledge), and the subconscious seems to blend into emotions which are as much physiological as they are mental. Recollective memory is recall into consciousness, and is fallible and incomplete, but without recall we would have no capacity to act to any purpose. And there is memory which is not recollective. Our experience of being the person we are comes to us as derived from the past, often as an association of emotions. Moreover, our experience of our present selves as arising out of our past does not come as a single linear strand. The influences are multiple, various, and entangled.[6]

So memory gives us ourselves as derived from the past. We know that some of the properties of our present experience depend on experiences we have just had; when we hear the notes *do re*, we hear *re* as higher because we have just heard *do*[7], and we should not hear dissonances if a note we had just heard did not carry over into the note we are immediately hearing. This direct experience of a carry-over affects the character of what is present.

B. F. Skinner[8] says that words relating present behaviour to past and future events should be eschewed, as importing more than bare Stimulus–Response. So 'the term "try" must be rejected, because it implies the relation of a given sample of behaviour to past and future events; but the term "walk" may be retained because it does not. The term "see" must be rejected, but "look toward" may be retained because "see" implies more than turning the eyes towards a source of stimulation.' I owe the reference to Mary Midgley, who observes that 'walk' and 'look towards' also have implications from the past if there are to be actions. One might say that Skinner is leaving us with what Santayana called 'the solipsism of the present moment'. Moreover, response to a stimulus can be shown to be not just a single isolated reaction, but to be affected by previous excitations and a multitude of other conditions in the organism.[9]

We cannot doubt that our present life is shaped by past experiences. In the case of habit memory, this shapes behaviour in what is also a physiological entraining of the body. Memory which is conscious recall is another matter, and is notoriously selective. In such memory it is as though one opened now one door, now another, in a house in which one once lived, and where most of the doors are shut. The house is full of ghosts; one hears voices, and sometimes one can trace where they come from and sometimes not.

>*Wenn die Uhren so nah*
>*wie im eigenen Herzen schlagen,*
>*und die Dinge mit zagen*
>*Stimmen sich fragen:*
>*Bist du da? — :*
>*dann bin ich nicht der, der am Morgen erwacht,*
>*einen Namen schenkt mir die Nacht,*
>*den keiner, den ich am Tage sprach,*
>*ohne tiefes Fürchten erführe —*
>*Jede Türe*
>*in mir gibt nach . . .*
>*Und da weiß ich, daß nichts vergeht,*
>*Keine Geste und kein Gebet*
>*(dazu sind die Dinge zu schwer),*
>*meine ganze Kindheit steht*
>*immer um mich her.*
>*Niemals bin ich allein.*
>*Viele, die vor mir lebten*
>*und fort von mir strebten,*
>*webten,*
>*webten*
>*an meinem Sein.*
>*Und setz ich mich zu dir her*
>*und sage dir leise: Ich litt-*
>*hörst du?*
> *Wer weiß wer*
> *murmelt es mit.*[10]

When the clocks strike so close as though they were in one's own heart and things ask with shy voices 'Are you here?' Then I am not the one who awoke this morning, the night gave me a name which no one to whom I talked during the day could learn without deep fear. Each door in me gives way. And in that moment I know that nothing passes away, no gesture and no prayer (things are too weighty for that to happen). My whole childhood surrounds me, I am never alone. Many who lived before me, many who strove away from me, were weaving, weaving my life.

And when I sit down near you and quietly say: I suffered — do you hear me?

Rilke can put this sense of the presence of the past into poetry. Since we do not really know how memories are stored, nor how they shape our present experiences, I do not know how to put this in unequivocal prose. Yet I know that I have this inheritance from the past and that it effects my present state. On the model of causation as a sequence of events, a present state succeeds a past state, and that is all there is to be said. But memory suggests there is a great deal more to be said. What has happened in the past has had real effects in making us what we are – though we can do something about the use we make of it, and this can give us hope.

I do not understand how memory works (and I am not sure that anyone does). It might all be transeunt causation if there were a coherent story of a causal chain from external stimulus to response – to laying down of a neural trace – to the arousal of the trace – to a conscious memory. This starts transeuntly, and it goes on in a story, which may possibly be true of habit memories (except that the entraining of them is likely to involve more than neural traces). In recollected memory it is as though we were aware of our present state of consciousness as activated in complexes of thoughts and feelings, some of which we refer to the past. In remembering, say, a poem we may have completely forgotten when and how we learnt it; this is of no interest. What matters is the memory energising as immanent in our present conscious experience.

I am pretty sure that memory does not work through a scanner decoding neural traces laid down by past stimuli, one for each. Memories are too kaleidoscopic, and do not appear to be so closely localised; after brain surgery, functions which were thought to be connected with excised bits of the brain can get taken over by others, and apparently lost memories can be recovered. It looks rather as though the organism is an imminded body[11] which is a carrier of cumulative experience. In habit memory, there is an entraining of the body; the plaguing involuntary memory where one has a tune running in the head may be a form of habit memory. Recollected memory is a form of conscious thinking; and consciousness can free itself from the present moment, anticipating the future speculatively and re-enacting the past in thought. What one remembers can be a matter of what interests one and interest will have an element of affective concern, which may be why old people have such good long-term memories, but lose their intermediate memories, and may even be unsure of short-term memories. The affective concern can continue and accumulate without the recollected memory, as in anxiety; to find a way of recall can then be a means of understanding the concern and getting it into perspective. So the problem of memory goes with that of consciousness. We cannot (at present at any rate) explain either, but can give a phenomenology of the forms they take. The more memory is habit, the more it seems bound up with a functioning of the physiological organism. The more it is conscious recall, the more it can be free ranging; still, I believe, working through the psycho–physiological organism, but taking control and not being controlled by it.

I cannot pretend to know how this happens, or how inheritance from the past gets transmitted through the psycho–physiological organism into the present. Apart from the transeunt cause from which the memory starts, I have put it under the heading of immanent causation. 'Immanent causation' was used where the product of an activity was not separable from the producing activity; the activity of remembering is not distinguishable from the memory which is its product. There is indeed a harking back to some event or experience in the past; but there is no recognisable succession of actions and reactions in a causal chain leading up to the memory. Immanent causation was used of changes in a system where no such succession of separate actions and reactions can be traced. There is none the less a modification of the system, and this can have non-reversible earlier and later phases. For these reasons I find it appropriate to speak of memory in terms of immanent and not of transeunt causation. I recognise that 'immanent causation' is a descriptive term rather than an explanatory one, since, except perhaps where changes in a system can be formulated mathematically, it does not refer to a *modus operandi* which shows how the system functions. Nevertheless, it may not be without value to emphasise that there is such a functioning, and to try to describe it.

My original concern, however, is with the fact that our experience comes to us not instantaneously, but as derived from the past. Transition from the past, particularly from the immediate past, is built into it. There is persistence from one phase to another, the earlier phase passing over into the later one. This is so inescapable a part of our experience that we take it for granted. If we do not take it for granted, but reflect on the processes of nature as we experience them, these appear not as separate chunks of events in successions, but as transitions where there is no sharp boundary between past, present, and future. It is more likely that the boundaries we give events are drawn in our theoretic interpretations than that the transitions are interpretations we put on our experiences, and are not there in the actual processes of nature out of which our experiences come. Without transitions, there would be a Zeno universe. I do not see how we could live in a Zeno Universe, and short term memory is a testimony that we do not.

Where so little is known as to how memory actually works, to use it in trying to throw light on causation appears as illuminating *obscurum per obscurius*. But we can at any rate hold to the fact that memory gives us an inescapable experience of the present as derived from the past, which is in general reliable, even if a particular memory may be shown to be mistaken. Moreover, present experience not only comes as arising out of the immediate past, but it also points forward in anticipation of the immediate future. We may be told that we should cultivate experiences of living in the immediate present – but how immediate is this? At any rate it would be a state in which the activities of life would be suspended.

10 Immanent Causation in Organisms and in Body—Mind

In the memory which is recall, inheritance is also appropriation which can be put to new use. In habit memory, inheritance comes as entrained repetition of a pattern. Recall memory belongs to our conscious experience, habit memory is part of the psycho—physiological substructure of our experience. I do not know how far down into nature habit memory, or some analogy with it, may go. If it can be extended, I suspect that the notion of a functioning organism would also need to be extended with it. To press this could lead to pan-psychism, which might be avoided if 'memory' is divested of any suggestion of conscious awareness, and used for a store of cumulated phylogenetic inheritance on which the individual draws in ontogeny.[1] This, it may be claimed, is shown by the way in which the embryo runs through a repertoire of evolutionary forms.

If memory is extended to physiological 'memory', where evolutionary inheritance is recapitulated in a developing organism, and if we are not to read back a form of mental experience into this, the analogy with memory must be a way of interpreting something clearly characteristic of organic life.

Organic life has two aspects on which we can fasten – development and functioning. Development is a process in which a pattern is emerging and not just repeated; the different stages are continuous, even if some of them also happen in bursts. Functioning is the contribution one part makes in relation to others in the maintenance of a system. It can also refer to the working of the system as a whole. Both development and functioning take time. One part functions in relation to others in a systematic complex; one stage in development is dependent on the stage before. Moreover, even the most Aristotelian-minded upholder of the notion of development as the actualising of potentiality must know that

96

this is not just an individual unfolding itself. The developing individual is sustained in an environment (and this includes getting its sustenance). Some of these transactions are describable as transeunt causation; some of them appear as changes in the system as a whole, where the product is not separable from the producing activity. Sometimes changes in a system can be broken down into the action of its parts on each other; but sometimes, it would seem, not. Possibly (I say this with every hesitation) the changes in fundamental particles might be an extreme case of the latter. Particles are destroyed or exchanged for others where no discernible transeunt causation is discernible. This is said therefore to be a breakdown of causation. It might be an irreducible form of immanent causation in their transformations.

Immanent causation might, then, have an application in the world of quantum mechanics. I feel on surer ground in saying it has an application in the organic world. What would be more significant would be if there could be a generalised notion of organism through which immanent causation applied to both.

Whitehead said in *Science and the Modern World*[2] that science is becoming the study of organisms. 'Biology is the study of the larger organisms; whereas physics is the study of the smaller organisms.' It was this generalised notion of organism which some of us hoped to find developed in his later work and we were disappointed. In *The Principles of Natural Knowledge* he defined primary organisms as 'unities functioning and with spatio—temporal extensions'.[3] The basic conception is that there is a *unit* with a time-span, and it *functions* with spatio—temporal extension, and this is said to hold of the ultimate units of physics (perhaps fundamental particles as energetic systems), as also of biological organisms.

One way of describing these basic units was given by Whitehead in his middle-period writings under what he called 'non-uniform objects'.[4] 'Uniform objects' require no minimum quantum of time-lapse. A 'material object' such as a chair is a uniform object; any slice of the events making up its history can be recognisable as that chair, so that it is possible to think of it as existing 'at a given moment'.[5] A non-uniform object is one which needs a minimum time-span in order to display the character at all. A simple instance is a wave. There is no wave at an instant, and a wave is only at a point in the sense of passing a point determined by other local things. A wave displays a pattern with a periodicity from trough to crest to trough. Such a non-uniform object has patterned segments with time intervals in an on-going process, and the pattern is reiterated and carried forward unless it is cancelled by interference from another wave with the same periodicity, but out of phase with it. Thus 'non-uniform objects' provide non-arbitrary segments of a process where the pattern is carried forward from one segment to the next. Whitehead thinks that the fundamental constituents of nature are likely to be non-uniform objects, with vibratory or oscillatory patterns.[6] This might, I think, help towards a view of continuity as a transmission of pattern from one stage of a process to another. It might help, because it would show the 'passage of nature' as structured by patterned units which need time to be those units, and where the pattern is reiterated from one unit to another. The pattern is not only repeated but carried over. Carrying over does not take place at an instant; it involves derivation from the past and direction towards the future.

I have referred to the letter in which Whitehead said that it was wrong to represent his view as just transfer of character. It was transfer, he said, of 'subjective form', effected by 'conformal feeling'. 'Subjective form' is how a feeling is experienced at one stage, then conformed to in a feeling at the next. I do not want to use this psycho–physiological language of 'feelings'; I find its subjectivity unhelpful. However, I think Whitehead's view of a pattern getting carried over can be detached from the philosophy of his later books. (In the later books the process becomes one of picking up rather than carrying over; this is another story, and not one which I find plausible.) In the earlier books, he sees the persistence of an 'enduring object' in the reiteration of pattern carried forward in an on-going process. In physics, he sees this as one in which the ultimate constituents of nature propagate their energy in wave-like transmissions over space and time. A wave, with its periodicity has such a reiterated pattern. In the case of a biological organism, there is not only the reiteration of pattern, but there is its *replication* in new organisms.[7] That reiteration can become replication may be the crucial first distinction between the physical and the biological. It is not an absolute distinction, in that it can be said to happen in the growth of crystals in a solution. But in the biological case, the replicated units become detached from the propagating unit (or units where there is sexual reproduction). The distinction between reiteration in stages of the history of one continuant and replication into other continuants is a mark of 'living organisms'; it can be applied as a criterion for viruses, which are usually thought of, at any rate as of now, as the nearest we have to the borderline between the living and non-living. Viruses replicate, all too rapidly for our comfort, in the medium of host cells.

So persistence of pattern happens in replicated units which separate off from the original continuant to form new continuants. Here the notion of 'propagation' is properly at home, and it is more natural to see this as causal. The successor units have been propagated by the parent unit, or units where organisms reproduce sexually. New units bud off, and they carry an inheritance. This inheritance may be carried through genetic factors, but their role in the developing organism depends on other factors, internal and external. The organism as a whole is a system with a patterned development. Each organism is a functioning system, persisting over a time span, with its growth, maturation, senescence and death. Where one component in the organism can be distinguished as acting on others, this can be seen as transeunt causation. Immanent causation would be in the self-maintenance and growth of the system functioning as a whole. It may not sound as though this kind of causation had much explanatory power, but it is less like something invoked *ad hoc* for living organisms if it can be connected, as I have tried to connect it, with a more general view of the persistence of patterned systems in nature.

In A *New Science of Life: the Hypothesis of Formative Causation*[8] A. R. Sheldrake has put forward a view of what he calls 'formative causation'. Besides 'energetic causation', the mechanisms of which are increasingly discovered in physics and chemistry, and which are shown in the probabilistic outcomes of exchanges of energy, there is 'formative causation', by which natural systems get their organised patterns ('natural systems' here including atoms, molecules, crystals, as well as living organisms). Sheldrake claims that each system has the organisation it has because others of the same kind had it before, and it is transmitted through a 'morphogenetic field' across space and time from earlier specimens to their successors. This differs from my distinction of transeunt and immanent causation. His formative causation would be transeunt, since it involves factors working on a system from outside. The system 'resonates' with these, which are others of the same kind in the past. Of course there must already be some structure for any selective action to be possible. Sheldrake says each system has a 'morphogenetic germ', for instance a fertilised egg or the nucleus of an atom, which resonates with predecessors in a morphogenetic field. 'Formative causation' cannot then be a view of the origin of organisation. There is also the question of the relation of forms and fields, and of the meaning of 'resonance' in a morphogenetic field. I should see 'formative causation' in a process of internal development within a system, and not as working on it from outside. The former could be creative in a way in which the latter would not be. I see it working as a non-random tendency within a system, establishing and maintaining structures, and as internal to the same process as can be measured externally in 'energetic causation'. This internal directedness means that I have to allow an element of teleology in my immanent causation.

'Immanent causation', as used by W. E. Johnson, meant change or transformation within a system, where the change is not fully describable through the action on each other of separate items, either external to the system or as constituents within it. Immanent causation in a living system may indeed call for interactions between constituents in the system, but these take place within an overall pattern of development. Artifacts have an overall pattern in which regulators can be built in to counteract a limited number of foreseeable kinds of disturbance and aberration: while in a living system there is resilience through many co-ordinated internal adjustments meeting an indefinite number of kinds of threats, some of which of course will defeat it. A living system is also an open system, maintaining a steady state by repairing its losses of energy through intake of energy from the environment. In the end its powers of resilience, resistance, renewal are insufficient, and there is the onset (as yet little understood) of senescence, and finally death. A living system acts through the hierarchy of its sub-systems – through molecules, cells, and its endocrine, respiratory, and circulatory, and in higher organisms, nervous systems – maintaining and renewing itself as an integrated and integrating unity. Vitalistic views ascribe this activity to a distinct factor, an entelechy, acting on and organising the other components of the system. Apart from the fact that this factor is not isolable, its acting on the physical body presents a difficulty analogous to that of something purely mental acting causally on a purely physical body. This cannot be summarily dismissed on the grounds that like can only cause like – the notion of cause is too many sided to be put under such *a priori* constraints. The real difficulty is experiential. We do not experience ourselves as ghosts in machines, whether intellectual ghosts, or managerial ghosts pushing the molecules round in our bodies. We experience ourselves as embodied in our feelings, sensations and actions which take shape through the organism. Even in our thinking, the strongest candidate for something purely mental, we use language, with its tones, rhythms, articulations – physical sounds and shapes in which we 'express ourselves'.

To emphasise embodiment need not make one physicalist, still less materialist. The organism is a medium for the expression of living, and in some cases intelligent activity (one need only think of how this is shown in the physiognomy of facial expression). I am not prepared to say how far down the scale of living organisms some form of intelligent activity may extend. There are ranges of problem solving, not to be dismissed just as 'trial and error' if this means making purely random shots. There is groping, perhaps even by the amoeba putting out its pseudopods; searching, rather than just reacting to what meets it.

In spite of the romantic way such views are sometimes presented, I favour an 'organismic' rather than a vitalistic or mechanistic view.[9] A living system comes into action as a whole, and the macro-system uses its array of micro-systems. What about non-living systems? I have indicated sympathy with Whitehead's view that we should have an enlarged concept of 'organism', and a view of nature which extend this into what he called, in *Science and the Modern World*, 'organic mechanism'. This pre-dated the pan-psychism which people have found in his later works, though Whitehead himself repudiated the label of 'pan-psychist'. The 'mental pole' he ascribed to any organism stood for the possibility of establishing a new pattern of functioning, and was certainly not, except in what he called 'high-grade organisms', to be thought of as in any degree conscious. In fact, he played the role of consciousness down rather than played it up. Be this as it may, my interest is in his generalised view of organisms as 'unities functioning and with spatio-temporal extensions',[10] each going on in a patterned form of activity which reiterates the past pattern, and which sometimes jumps and settles into a new one. This would, I think, allow for the evolution of different kinds of system throughout nature, and for interrelations in networks of systems. There may be basic patterns (Laws of Nature?) which constrain what kinds of systems are possible, but I do not think of nature (or the universe), as some idealists have done, as a single overall organic system, itself an organism. I am, however, sympathetic to the thought that it may be the field of a basic activity channelled through individual organisms, and expressed through modes of functioning.

'Functioning' is a working together of parts in a system. That some part performs a 'function' means that its working has consequences either in contributing to the maintenance of the system, or to carrying out the tasks which it can perform when in working order. So if it is said that the function of the beating of the heart is to circulate the blood, this means more than just that the beating of the heart has the consequence that the blood circulates; it says that this consequence happens within a system where the working of one part regulates the working of others. (This is most apparent where there are corrective regulating devices, 'feed-backs'.) This is not conscious purposive teleology.[11] There can be a functioning of parts in a system which is a man-made artifact; here the functioning is set in the context of something designed for a purpose external to it. In the case of the organism, the functioning appears as internal mutual adjustments regulating the working of the parts, and in the case of disturbances, restoring equilibrium, or settling into a new equilibrium.

There is of course a large literature on this kind of biological teleology (if it is properly called 'teleology'). It describes a form of systematic unity in which the functioning of the parts in mutual regulation maintains the system and which also develops it in an on-going process over time to a maturation state. Perhaps no one has as yet succeeded in saying just what this 'teleology' is, as distinct from the teleology of conscious purpose;[12] it centres on the self-maintenance and persistence over a period of a system which is also an on-going process. The self-maintenance and persistence of the system is of course dependent on its interaction with an environment, but it is a unit with its own boundary within this environment.

In the paper 'The living system: determinism stratified'[13] Professor Paul Weiss gives the clearest description I know of organisms as dynamic networks of interactions and not bundles of precisely programmed linear causal chains. ('Determinism' in his title stands for there being determinable correlations and configurations at the macro-level, in spite of many of the movements of the elements at the micro-level being indeterminable. It does not, I think, stand for a hard-line determinism.) The functioning of an organic system at the macro-level is not just the sum of single track component processes, and it shows much less variance than these. Organisms are 'relatively stable complexes of functional and structural properties mutually related through matrices of less well-defined more fleeting configurations'. If the pattern were the resultant just of the random action of the sub-components, it would be likely to be obliterated rather than maintained.

I believe, therefore, that one needs to speak of integration in processes of growth and development, and also of directedness towards goals internal to these, for instance in seeking food; ways of pursuing these goals can be varied when one is blocked. If this is a 'teleology', it is one internal to the development of the organism, not one of taking means to an external end. I think something like integration and development must be allowed; (there are certainly better ways of putting it, than I have found and we hope to be able to understand more about how these processes work). The improbability of these orderly results being achieved as the outcome of an assemblage of random processes would be so vast that I do not think it would be rational to accept it. Also in a random world, one would expect such organised systems to be extremely rare, and yet we see them round us all the time.

A philosopher with a view which might be relevant to this was C. S. Peirce. He saw *habit formation* as a general tendency in nature: indeed he said that 'the hypothesis suggested by the present writer is that all laws are results of evolution; that underlying all other laws is the only tendency which can grow by its own virtue, the tendency of all things to take habits'.[14] He calls it 'Lamarckian'; but it may be wider:

> Lamarckian evolution is thus evolution by the force of habit. — That sentence slipped off my pen while one of those neighbors whose function in the social cosmos seems to be that of an Interrupter was asking me a question. Of course, it is nonsense. Habit is mere inertia, a resting on one's oars, not a propulsion. Now it is energetic projaculation (lucky there is such a word, or this untried hand might have been put to inventing one) by which in the typical instances of Lamarckian evolution the new elements of form are first created. Habit, however, forces them to take practical shapes, compatible with the structures they affect, and, in the form of heredity and otherwise, gradually replaces the spontaneous energy that sustains them. Thus, habit plays a double part; it serves to establish the new features, and also to bring them into harmony with the general morphology and function of the animals and plants to which they belong.[15]

'Habit' here stands for something acquired, not just for any regular form of behaviour. Habit is an entrainment which can continue without attention. It is, as Peirce says, a form of inertia. But habits get formed and continue within existing structured settings, so I do not see how habit can carry the whole weight of providing structures. In the second passage quoted, Peirce recognises the need for a setting as well as the need for what he calls 'energetic projaculation'. He sees habit as the entraining and imprinting of an acquired pattern. It may be that in the organism that answers most closely to memory.

Whether or not memory and habit extend back into all evolutionary nature, at any rate they are conditions for human action. In action we depend on short-term memory of the immediate past to do anything purposive at all; we generally depend on memory of the remoter past to do anything which might be sensible in the situation in which we find ourselves, and we depend on habitual skills to carry out the movements necessary for doing it. Actions, I have already said, are bodily movements, but this is more than just being movements of bodies. To say what more brings us into the well-worn territory of 'Mind and Body'. I do not intend to enter further into this than may be needed to stake out a claim that their relation may be one of immanent causation.

Such a view will have to start from the intimate interconnection we find between what we call states of mind and physiological states. States of mind can affect metabolic changes in the body, as by the secretion of adrenalin in a state of fear; and the ingestion of drugs can affect states of mind. To our intuitive experience, emotions are outstanding examples of states which are both mental and physiological. Intuitive experience need not be sacrosanct, but in this case there is experimental evidence to support it. Bio-feedback machines can monitor (and measure) physiological changes which ensue when a subject gets into a mentally relaxed state, or, more significantly, since relaxation is obviously also a physical state, when he entertains certain ideas. 'It has been found that heart rate, blood pressure, brain waves, muscles (and probably much more) of the physiologic being all react to dirty words.'[16] One might think that the day had now gone by when dirty words could so much as bring a blush to a maiden's cheek; but there are plenty of other examples; I have mentioned the secretion of adrenalin when something is said which alarms us.

If perceptions of meaning affect physiological states, this can be a problem for the more radical forms of the now fashionable physicalism. Kathleen Wilkes, in her recent book *Physicalism*,[17] is well aware of this. She presents Physicalism not as 'metaphysical monism', (a view that there is only one kind of thing) but as a view of a type of explanation; explanations of actions should in the end be capable of being given exhaustively in terms appropriate to the physical sciences. These would not use intensional terms, such as 'want', 'belief', 'purpose'. She accepts that such intensional terms may have their use in talking about actions on the macro-level, but at the micro-level explanation should be refined down to neural events. ('Should be' because admittedly this would call for a neurophysiology far beyond any we now have). Nevertheless, even if psychological language with intensional terms denoting conscious states is used on the macro-level, consciousness would still only be 'epiphenomenal' (the current term is 'supervenient'). We can tell stories about conscious states, but the conscious states have no role in what is actually going on.

I have fallen back here into a substantive way of talking; I think that however much a view like Kathleen Wilkes' may claim to be about kinds of explanation, and not about 'the relation of Mind and Body', yet to say that the ultimate explanation should be physicalist suggests that what are being explained are in the end physical events or physical realities. I think Robert Kirk is right here in his article 'From Physical Explicability to Full-Bodied Materialism;[18] he argues that the notion of physical explicability entails that all true mental target sentences will be implied by the true physical sentences. A target sentence is one whose falsity raises no problem for materialism, but whose truth might be thought to do so, for example 'Socrates has a greenish after-image'. Non-target sentences are those whose truth or falsity would be irrelevant to the issue. This fastens on the *truth* of these sentences. The question of substantive truth is evaded if there are simply two stories in the formal mode, or two descriptions, physical and mental. Why need we be interested in the stories or in the descriptions unless we are interested in what they are about? And if one story or description is said to be basic, will not this mean that whatever it is about is also thought of as basic? If neither description is basic, and if both are said just to be distinct stories, does this not suggest that they are about two orders of events as happenings in two kinds of thing, neither of which is reducible to the other? Then in the substantive mode we get mental and physical parallelism, where neither can affect the other, just as in the formal mode the two stories must be kept distinct.

A view of mind—body as a unity with different levels of functioning which affect each other is one I find more plausible than radical dualism, epiphenomenalism, or mind—body parallelism. What kind of unity? A system in which there are physico—chemical states to which conscious states make a difference? Yes, so long as we do not talk of a conscious state, or indeed of consciousness, as if it were something on its own, and then speak of the body, or more likely the brain, as 'the seat of consciousness'. Austin Farrer in *The Freedom of the Will*[19] (one of the best books on the Mind—Body problem I know) remarks that 'consciousness cannot sit down, not having the wherewithal'. Rather, the whole sentient organism can become the instrument of a consciously directed, intelligent activity.[20] There may be nodal regions for the functioning of this, notably in the brain and nervous system. But we see intelligent activity in the movements of a violin player's fingers and in a tennis player's turn of the wrist. This is surely not only conscious thought transmitting messages from the brain to the hand – the co-ordinated activity is intelligently performed through the play of the whole body. If there is a neurological event in the brain which is the starter triggering off all this delicate co-ordination, it is certainly not something on which we can concentrate, nor (if it is indeed the starter of the activity) are we even aware of it.

This is where I think the otherwise attractive view of mental capacities as *emergent* properties fails to satisfy in its usual form. Emergence is in general the view that wholes, composed of constituents (say) A, B, C, in relation R will display properties which cannot be deduced simply from knowledge of the properties A, B, and C not so ordered, or in wholes not of the form $R(A, B, C)$.[21] Put in this way, the emergents could be seen as Gestalt properties of organised wholes, and there is nothing surprising in saying that an ordered whole will have properties not deducible from those of its constituent parts when not so ordered. If we call certain functionings of an organism emergent capacities, we do not only want to say that they are properties displayed by the organism as a whole, and not deducible from a knowledge of its constituent parts. We also want to be able to say that the higher level capacities can work on or perhaps in the lower level ones, not only making use of them instrumentally, but in some cases affecting how they function.[22] The emotion of fear can be aroused by understanding something said to one, and it can cause the adrenalin to flow. Fear may not be a very high-grade state of mind, and there can be cases where a higher-grade activity (or mental states) can influence a physico—chemical state of the body — as when healing processes are promoted or hastened by getting into certain states of concentration or relaxation. In such cases we speak popularly of the action of Mind on Matter. Gilbert Ryle in a well-known passage in *The Concept of Mind* called this way of talking a 'category mistake'.[23] He gave as an example of a category mistake a visitor to Oxford seeing the colleges, the museum, the Bodleian Library, and asking 'Where is the University?' The University, the visitor must realise, is not another member of this set; 'it is just the way in which all that he has already seen is organised'. I do not think this settles the question. True, the University is not one more member of the class of the institutions the visitor has seen, but there are things like the conferring of degrees which are done by the University through its accredited agents, and such things are not just ways the colleges, the Library and the Museum are organised. Indeed, if we are to be fussy about visible buildings, the University has a special one, the Registry, though this is perhaps not an *argumentum ad hominem* to Gilbert Ryle; no one would say the Registry was the University, though it is its administrative office. So 'the University' is not just a name describing the organisation of the colleges and other visible institutions; things are done and decisions made in its name which affect them. Here again we see that we do not only want properties of ordered wholes, but to see how ways of functioning at one level affect the functioning at others. We need not only order, but efficacy. I do not think that Gilbert Ryle, with his strong interest in intelligent skills, would have disputed this. What he was disputing was that the mind could be classified as a substantive thing, along with the body as another substantive thing. I agree with him in not wanting to run this kind of dualist view of mind and body. I should put the question in terms of how higher-level functionings in the organism can work on lower-level functionings, as well as the lower-level ones affecting the functioning of the high-level ones.

We have different processes modifying each other. Some of these are interactions which can be understood in chemical terms such as the digestion of food and its metabolism in the tissues of the body. The energy supplied through this can then get used in higher grade functionings, such as composing or performing a sonata or writing a book. In such performance, the higher-grade activity happens through the organism as its vehicle, until in turn one of the lower-level functionings reacts back, perhaps as hunger pains or sleepiness, though even these can be ignored for a time if we are really concentrating on what we are doing. So a higher-level functioning, not measurable as exchanges of energy, has discernible effects not only on motor functions (we can get up and walk) but on chemical metabolism. An intelligent activity takes shape through the organism. Its hold is incomplete, because other processes in the organism have their own requirements. Nevertheless, within these limitations, the organism becomes a medium of intelligent activity.

Intelligent activity takes effect through a series of bodily movements and directs some of these. Can this be seen as a form of immanent causation? It is not transeunt causation where there is the external action of a distinguishable factor. Neither is it just immanent causation as change within a system as a whole; nor is it just the persistence of the system into a further stage. There is mutual affecting of the 'mental' and the 'physical', but not as a regular functional co-variance, and it can be episodic rather than continuous. If it is called 'immanent causation', this would be in more like the original (metaphorical?) sense of one activity 'in-dwelling' another and being expressed through it. I spoke earlier of 'levels' of functioning; this is another metaphorical term, and misleading if it suggests a hierarchy with spatial tiers. It can be used to indicate that what we call 'higher' capacities can find their own expression through 'lower' ones, but also are dependent on the working of 'lower' ones. 'Dependent' does not here have the sense given it as the dependent variable in a co-variant functional relation. Either the 'mental' or the 'physical' can be affected or can do the affecting, and in that sense be the independent variable. 'Dependent' here means that mental capacities operate through physical ones, whereas the 'lower' physical ones can go on without the higher 'mental' ones being exercised. (There may be a value judgement in the distinction of higher and lower, but that is not my concern here.) The 'higher' functionings (mental) need the 'lower' (physical) functionings, but they are not just supervenient on them, since they can make a difference to the working of the latter, notably in directing bodily movements; they can also modify some physiological functions through emotional states. (Such a dualist as Descartes did not quite know on which side to put the emotions.) The exercise of a 'mental' capacity can trigger off a physical one; yet the 'mental' is not 'higher' in the sense of always being in control, and can be inhibited, notably in loss of consciousness. Where 'mental' capacities issue in intelligent activity, a central directedness comes into play, and the organism identifies itself with it.

So I see an organism as a single system, some of whose activities are intelligent, and I should not want to draw a clear line between intelligent and non-intelligent organisms. There are surely forms of animal intelligence; and lower organisms may not only behave by stimulus and response, but may grope about, searching for ways round their problems. When we come to living systems which are bearers of intelligent activity, this groping can become free ranging, entertaining theoretical as well as practical possibilities. Here causal efficacy is not only a thrust from one stage to another in an on-going activity, where patterns are repeated, or modified through predictable and sometimes measurable operations. The input from one stage is drawn on in the production of something genuinely new, whether a problem-solving action, an intellectual idea, a work of art, or even a good joke (which is a minor work of art). This is creative causation, and we know that in some degree we are all capable of it. The more we see our own capacities as embodied capacities, and ourselves as not cut off in any absolute way from the rest of nature, the more I believe we shall need to think of creative power which comes up in us as also active in the ways open to them in other organic forms through nature. This would be a belief in a basic kind of immanent causation in organisms as active systems – a belief to which I find myself impelled by the undoubted fact of creativity.

POSTSCRIPT

My emphasis on embodiment, and on actions as expressed through bodily movements, could be taken as prejudging the issue over paranormal phenomena where causation does not appear to depend on physical contact. Notably, these include psychokinesis (the movement of bodies at a distance – is this by 'willing' them to move?), and telepathy (the transference of thoughts from one mind to another without physical communication).

I certainly do not want to exclude these. If causation in general means that the happening of one thing is (in part at least) dependent on something else, and if a cause is something which makes its effect more likely, these happenings could indeed indicate its working in some form. On my view I take 'makes' more seriously, and also say that the cause is efficacious in producing the effect. There is abundant anecdotal evidence of these happenings; as inductive evidence, these need to be repeatable, and in some cases they are. Inductive evidence supporting a causal explanation is strengthened where there is a law-like generalis- ation, which, if possible, should connect with others in a system; here these law-like statements are not at present forthcoming. The most hopeful approach to causal explanation at this stage is probably the experimental one, where alleged factors in an 'effect' situation can be produced or prevented.

I have tried to eschew *a priori* constraints on causation, such as that every event has a cause, that every event is determined by a sufficient cause, and that like can only be caused by like. However, I find it very difficult to resist the notion that, though a factor spatially and temporally separated from the effect may be selected and called the cause, there will be intermediaries leading up to the effect. Yet gravity is a force acting at a distance. I find myself disposed to want some kind of field through which this takes place. But if there is a field in which paranormal action takes place, no numbers can at present be assigned to it, as they can in the gravitational and electro—magnetic fields. I stand by my view that we act on other things through our bodily movements. What I am not sure about are the limits of the disturbances our bodies can produce in the environment, or what forces there may be in this environment besides those already recognised. Our bodily movements are localised in regions, but we do not know the exact boundaries of these regions. Localised activity of a certain kind in a region might extend through a field, and affect something entering into it which is susceptible to that kind of influence. 'Field' may of course be a metaphor here; I am casting round for a suggestion as to how, where such paranormal happenings are well supported, there could be causal links between them.

I believe that such happenings will call for an enlarged view of the psycho–physiological capacities of organisms, and especially those organisms we call 'persons'; also of the relations between particular organisms and others in the environment. Nothing in what I have said is intended to preclude an enlarged view; indeed I hope my approach is one which makes room for it. The term 'Body–Mind' in the heading of this chapter is designed to indicate the unity of the thinking living organism. It is not designed to indicate an epiphenomenalist view in which thinking capacities have no causal initiative.

11 Efficacious Grace

'Immanence' is, of course, a word normally used of what is called divine 'indwelling'. I have been using it in a general sense for changes involving growth, development, activity within a system, where this is not explained through the transeunt causation of something acting externally on something else. Now I shall be even more expressly metaphysical, and try to speak of immanent divine causation. Indeed, if it is possible to speak at all of divine causation, this is where I should want to start.

It may not be possible to speak meaningfully of divine causation. Causation, in the ways in which I have been looking at it as efficacious, stands for a propensity in things to produce effects, and as explanatory it is used under restrictions, where causal factors operate in contexts of other conditions. A divine cause has been thought of as context free. A First Cause is said to be not just the first member of a linear chain of causes and effects; it is unlike any ensuing members, and has been called self-caused – *causa sui*. More often, within the tradition, it is said to be uncaused, a necessary being; if it exists, it is impossible for it not to have existed. This is necessity *de re* in the strongest possible form. Such necessity as I have allowed in causation has been not *de re*, but within deductions from generalisations where these are used in causal explanations. Divine Causation which invokes a First Cause or Necessary Being apart from the world will not have this kind of necessity. It cannot be seen as instantiating a general law. Nor could it be a Mackian INUS condition, one that is insufficient but necessary in a set of conditions which are unnecessary but sufficient for the effect. Moreover, an INUS condition need not be unique; it can be selected according to our interest in what aspect of a situation we want to explain. Cause, as I have seen it, is a selective notion; it can be explanatory within a context, but it does not give a total explanation. Mill tried to make it total by saying that a causal explanation would cite all the necessary antecedents, but such a composition would not be any kind of causal explanation we could use. In any case, it could hardly be a theistic explanation, even supposing multiple causes as in Hume's committee of minor deities. A First Cause would (analytically) be single, and also unique. As unique, it could not instantiate any general law, and so its use in explanation could not fit that model.

This is not, however, the only model. I have allowed explanation by agency causation, and this is the form that an appeal to Divine Causation to explain the world has usually taken. The expression used of agency causation – 'making things happen' – might then be said to be particularly appropriate.

If we look for an agency view here, it would I think, have to be a von Wright one. The agent does something which sets a system in motion, or inserts an event which can be a cause. I have suggested that von Wright, by putting the action of the agent outside the causal sequence, seems to be describing things as being made to happen by fiat. Von Wright's view would, of course, not let one speak of the divine action as a *cause*, since he puts actions outside causal sequences, which are sequences of events. I have said why I am dissatisfied with his view that actions are not causes. However, in this context one might accept it as a way of saying that the First Cause is not causal in the same sense as secondary causes. This might well fit a traditional view of divine caustion. Not only is the First Cause not a cause in the sense given in the sequences of what are called secondary causes; also it does not operate by acting on anything else, because, until it has produced something, there is nothing to operate on. The Judaeo–Christian tradition has indeed spoken of divine creation as bringing about the world without anything to act upon: 'by the word of the Lord were the heavens made' – the outstanding case of creation by fiat.

There have been views which give divine action someting to act on, and so provide a context within which it is causative. Plato's Demiurge in the *Timaeus* fashions a world out of pre-existing inchoate material, and looks at eternal forms to see how to shape it. This would be agency causation to explain the formation of the world, but not its existence. In the Judaeo–Christian tradition its *existence* is said to be explained by a pure act of creation which does not need any context in which to operate. The being which is able to perform such a pure act is itself pure activity, uncaused, but a necessary and sufficient cause for any possible world. That any possible world depends on such a cause is a sense given to the word 'necessary'; it is not just that our actual world happens to have such a cause.

Philosophical theologians have devoted, and continue to devote, efforts to present arguments to explain the existence of the world. I confess, however, that I can never find them gripping, especially as a form of causal argument. I find them 'dialectical' in Kant's sense; they can be argued this way and that, and they run into antinomies. This seems to me particularly so of the modal arguments over possibility and necessity. St Ambrose said. *'Non in dialectica placuit Deus salvum facere populum suum'*. But if God did not want to save his people through dialectic, is it likely that he should do so through modal logic? (This would indeed be an unfair remark if those who seek through modal logic to establish the truth of the proposition that a necessary being must exist produced a proof. But I see their arguments as contained within formal schemes, and not as substantive proof.)

If we are to have a strong necessity *de re* to explain the world, the necessity would, I think, better apply to the whole world system, and not be confined to an external necessary being creating a contingent world. We should be back to Spinoza, or perhaps to Hegel, seeing the world as a necessary development. These are views not of transeunt but of immanent causation, and immanent causation is where I want to go, or at any rate to start. But I cannot go there in Spinoza's way, or in Hegel's. My world is too pluralistic and too open-ended to be a self-necessitating system.

Nevertheless, I think that to approach the question of divine causation by looking at actual forms of creative activity within the world can be more serious than trying to explain the world as a whole by reference to an external cause. Indeed, such a kind of explanation strikes me as Deistic rather than as Theistic. I do not use these terms to make a debating point with theologians, but to indicate that transeunt causation may not be satisfactory as a view of what philosophical theism has tried to say. Be that as it may, I find views of transeunt divine causation produce ideas to entertain, rather than to believe. They are, as I said, dialectical.

It may, of course, be said that they are ways of acknowledging Divine Transcendence. But it seems to me that the attributes of a transcendent Necessary Being are apt to be instances of what Whitehead called 'paying metaphysical compliments to God'. There are indeed motives for the compliments — the sense of reverence, of uniqueness, of a resistance to reductionist views by which the worship of God becomes a poetic way of talking about something else. These are motives to be respected, and the insistence on the notion of Divine Transcendence may be used to safeguard them. But I do not think they help us to understand divine causation.

So I turned to the notion of divine causation as immanent causation. Is this any more intelligible?.

With this in mind, I looked into the literature on Divine Immanence. I found that, though the term is often used, its meaning has hardly been seriously discussed. There is an article on the historical background by A. C. McGiffert in the *Encyclopedia of Religion and Ethics* (1914). He says (what I suspected) that the theological use of the words 'Transcendent' and 'Immanent' started in the 19th century, though they were used in various philosophical senses by Spinoza, Kant, and the Schoolmen (especially in the various senses of 'transcendental'). Significantly, he ends by saying that modern treatments have little philosophical or theological value. 'Problems emerge which are neither solved nor as a rule seriously grappled with'. Baldwin's *Dictionary of Philosophy and Psychology* (1901) has a short note, defining Immanence as the 'indwelling and inworking of Deity in nature and man'. There is no notice at all in the contemporary *Encyclopedia of Philosophy* of 1967.

J. R. Illingworth published a book called *Divine Immanence*[1] in 1898. In this it is said that matter is the medium through which spirit is expressed, and therefore matter is of use to spirit, but spirit is not of use to matter; matter is what it is apart from spirit. But since spirit uses it for its own expression, it is claimed that matter exists for the sake of spirit. (This is stated as apologetic rather than argued.) Helen Oppenheimer in *Immanence and Incarnation*[2] (1973) says that the notion of Immanence should be taken seriously, and interprets it as an internal relation between persons. 'Internal relation' has a number of meanings (A. C. Ewing in his *Idealism* listed ten of them).[3] Helen Oppenheimer takes an internal relation between persons as one in which each influences the other. I see 'immanence' as standing here for a more intimate relation than one between people who influence each other. It stands for one activity, power, spirit – whatever word we can use – indwelling and pervading another.[4] An analogy might be a chemical fusion of substances making a new substance. But here the different elements can be analysed and in principle they are separable, though in some cases this may have to await the discovery of new techniques such as electrolysis. But there is no way in which this can be done with the immanence of the divine in the human. The metaphors used of Immanence as internal may be as puzzling as the spatial metaphors used of Transcendence as 'external'. There are strong metaphors like 'breath', and more hidden ones in words like 'indwelling', 'participation', 'infusion', 'possession'.

My impression is that while the language of theology has mainly been that of Transcendence, the language of religious devotion has mainly been that of Immanence. Bradley fastened on this in the essay 'On God and the Absolute'.[5] Attacking (I think unanswerably) the notion of God as *a* person over against others, he went on to say that in living religion: 'the reality of God means his own actual presence within individual souls, and, apart from this presence, both he and they are no more than abstractions. Hence in genuine religion you have a "pantheism", which is not less there because it expresses itself by what in fact is an inconsistent polytheism.'

'Pantheism' has become a dirty word in philosophical theology. Rather than be afraid of it, we should look seriously at different things it might mean; this might help over the notion of Immanence. If Pantheism says that 'God is all', it is not the same as Immanence, since the latter suggests that God is within other things, so making a distinction which not made if we say that 'God is all'. 'God is all' (what John Laird in his underestimated Gifford Lectures, called 'totalitarian pantheism')[6] can be said to be a way of talking about the universe in religious language. This can indeed be one form of religious expression, where the object of devotion is the universe seen or felt as divine. Totalitarian pantheism is a form of double entry, where the same facts can be described alternatively in religious and in secular language. It can therefore be looked on as what Coleridge called 'painted atheism'.

Is the immanentist talk of 'indwelling power' more than double entry? It can be more, I think, if this power is seen as activating from within, but not identical with what it activates. I have said some hard things about divine causation as an explanatory notion on any known model of transeunt causation. But that there is a kind of divine causation which is effective through what in the theological literature is called 'grace' is something I can believe and live by. I shall turn therefore from the idea of transeunt causal explanation to that of efficacious grace, as a form of immanent causation.

To speak of Immanence is to say more than that the world in its totality is divine (Laird's 'totalitarian pantheism'). It also says more than that certain properties of everything in the world can be characterised as divine (what Laird called 'mitigated distributive pantheism').[7] It claims that these properties are as they are because of some operative power which is 'divinising' them. If we ask whether this 'comes from outside', which would make its operation a form of transeunt causation, we get into the assumptions of the spatial metaphors in transcendence. 'Inside' is not, I think, thus metaphorical, since the power *is* in us; the question is whether it is more than one of the powers of the mind. This brings us to the matter of causal initiative.

Let us postpone the question of source, and return to 'immanence' where one form of activity takes hold of another from within. Here 'the relation of mind and body' can provide an analogy, perhaps even an instance, for what we are looking for. Our experience of embodied activity gives us a more intimate feeling of living in the body than just inhabiting a house, or being a ghost in a machine. Bodily movements can carry intelligent activity which is given effect through them. Bodily processes make their own demands, with their drives and rhythms, and most of these do not come into consciousness. In intentional activity some bodily movements are consciously directed. I have said that such activity is not just an emergent Gestalt property of an organised system; it is an *activity*, a capacity, released indeed through the other levels of the system, but also taking initiative in acting through them. Action thus produces changes in the system as a whole, notably in directing its motion, and sometimes in affecting its chemical metabolism. This is immanent causation as change due to an operation within a system where the operant cannot be analysed as a distinct factor: one cannot say where the cause ends and the effect begins; one activity is causal as initiatory, but it fuses with the other which is the effect.

I have used the word 'operant', because intentional action is an initiative effecting changes, beginning with movements in the system, and, through these, in the external world. This initiative is characteristic of human action as causative. Can there be an initiative in what is called 'efficacious grace'?

Much religious teaching is concerned with conditions for the release of 'spiritual' power which can have a liberating and transforming – in religious language, a sanctifying – effect on other powers of mind and body. As intelligent activity can be expressed through physical activities, so it may be that 'efficacious grace' can be expressed through intelligent activities, including in these moral activities. Such spirituality – there is no satisfactory word for it – is not just a Gestalt property emerging from lower levels; it is operative in affecting these levels. 'Operative' is an efficacy word, and my interest in grace is in its being '*efficacious*'. If 'grace' is only a word which certifies a correct ecclesiastical status for certain offices or rituals, it is of no interest in thinking about efficacy as distinct from legal validity. J. L. Austin's expression 'performative words' has been misused in some discussions of these matters, notably in connection with sacraments. His definition of a performative utterance was of one which effects a result simply by virtue of something being said, either because of an institutional convention, as when a chairman closes a meeting by saying 'I declare the meeting closed', or because the pronouncement is itself the assuming of an obligation, as when to say 'I promise' is to make a promise. 'Performatory utterance' does not mean that certain words are causative in any sense other than that given them by understanding the conventions of such speech acts.

However, my interest is not in grace as something bestowed by the conventions of a speech act, but as something efficacious which can affect other powers of the embodied mind from within, and so be brought within a view of immanent causation. That there is power arising in the embodied mind which can be sustaining, renewing, sometimes also inspiring, is not, I think open to question. Whether it comes from 'outside' us is perhaps something we do not know; what we do know is that it comes and that we can respond to it.

I go back to what I have tried to say in general about the effectiveness of causes. We do not live in a world whose basic constituents are events which succeed each other, but do not change. We live in a world of operations, where participants in events act on each other and produce actual effects. (I have tried to argue this, and now ask just to be allowed to take it from there.) Some of these effects are changes measurable as exchanges of energy in transeunt causation; these are described by mechanisms, 'mechanism' being strictly a word for a *modus operandi* explained through the laws of mechanics. (Sometimes, of course 'mechanism' is used loosely to stand for any *modus operandi*.) Some changes – the overall growth of organisms, their searching behaviour, the use of memory in present experience – are not so explicable. They appear to come through a process in nature which is carried forward in the individual from stage to stage, establishing patterns, breaking them down, and establishing new ones by an internal integrating activity. Human creativity can be one spearhead of this, when the human individual used his biological inheritance and draws on his inheritance of memories to reach new patterns of action and thought.

Human creativity, I have said, arises out of a background of biological inheritance, and in intelligent activity it takes shape through bodily movements. This is how I have described the immanent causative action of mental activity and I have asked whether there could be an analogy here for the immanent causation of divine activity in the imminded body or embodied mind.

To look for the immanence of the divine in the world on the analogy of soul and body is an old story going back to the Greek philosophers. There, and notably with the Stoics, it could take the form of the notion of '*anima mundi*', the directive soul of the universe. For this to hold, we should need to be able to think of the universe as a total organism, directed by its soul. But can we do so? The universe may have an overall structure through laws such as gravity. But I do not think this makes the universe as a whole into a single organism. Here I agree with Austin Farrer's comment:

> The universe is indeed organized, or drawn together into unity; but it is so organized or drawn together a million million times over at all the single points where a field of forces finds a focus; and that is where any single active existence is present. All of these focal points have a certain extension – they are patterns of activity. Our own sentient animal existence is a highly-developed example. But to all evidence, there is no world-pattern pulling the universe together; it is pulled together by each of the infinite overlapping multitude of focal patterns, the patterns of actual and active existences.[8]

The formative action in the world is focused in individual centres, multiply related indeed, but still individual centres. And if we are looking here for immanent divine activity, we cannot evade the ghost of Schopenhauer. Schopenhauer calls power canalized in individual centres 'Will', but Will seen as restless striving which sets the individuals which are its instruments at odds with one another, and in the end destroys them. The only way to salvation is through renouncing activity and turning to pure contemplation, above all to aesthetic contemplation.

I think that Schopenhauer overdoes the cruelty and destructiveness in nature, but that is another story. The question is whether there is a further power in the mind able to overcome this ruthless self-seeking, and whether this can be continuous with, and responsive to a creative thrust which also comes up through nature. That the Will in human beings is a manifestation of a basic force of growth in nature was put by Margaret Masterman in a paper 'The Psychology of Levels of Will'.[9] This was quite independent of Schopenhauer, and described the Will as growth, taken psychologically, and growth as Will taken biologically. Will is not seen, as Schopenhauer saw it, as ruthless striving, which is in the end destructive, but as a deep power coming from what the old mystics called the *fundus* of the psyche. The spearhead of this is the growth into sanctity – Margaret Masterman quotes the phrase 'the terrible strength of the saints'. For Schopenhauer the spearhead was the creativity of superior gifted individuals, which can feed a ruthless daemonism: I have tried elsewhere to look at this as a problem within morality.[10] Here, in trying to speak of efficacious grace, I am concerned with the workings of a deep creative power which, instead of feeding a ruthless will to live, can feed a will to love, purifying the self-centredness of the will, where Schopenhauer could only see a remedy for self-centredness in its abnegation.

I have used the phrases 'will to live' and 'will to love'. This could be sentimental, unless we remember that love too can be ambivalent (as Schopenhauer saw), and unless there is a way through which it can be purified. This I take to be the concern of a good deal of spiritual training which not only finds that this happens, but that it is shown through behavioural signs. If the transforming power comes up through deep energies of the psyche, from a root where mental and physiological are hardly distinguished, it may indeed be the working in human life of a creative power which is also efficacious at other levels of nature in whatever forms are open to them.

We come back to the perennial question: is this an immanent divine power, or is it a power of nature in human life? If it is a natural power, then it is the more impossible to take a purely materialist view of nature. I believe that it is an initiating power, individualised in the many centres in which natural things exist. I do not think that this gives a causal explanation of the world in the sense of its being the effect of the transeunt action on it of an external cause. Its causation is of an immanent kind, which calls for our seeing nature teleologically, but in a teleology which takes shape internally in processes of development, rather than in a teleology which looks for means instrumental to an external end. Where this immanent causal activity, both formative and transformative in human life, is called 'grace', 'grace' is a word for efficacy and not for ritual validity.

I have said that I should be getting more metaphysical as I went on, and a view of causal efficacy in grace is very strongly metaphysical. Whether or no you will go as far as this, at least I hope that you will allow that we live in a universe in which we are actively interconnected through effective influences and operations. The influences are various; so too are the effects. Many are destructive, but some bring renewal and some a creative leap forward.

Notes and References

1 INTRODUCTION

1. I owe the report of this to R. B. Braithwaite, as a remark in conversation.
2. H. Kelsen, *Society and Nature* (London, 1946).
3. G. H. von Wright points out that *causa* in Latin was also a legal term (as in 'defending one's cause'), and the same he says is the case with the Finnish word *syy*. *Explanation and Understanding* (Ithaca, 1972) p. 65.
4. See 'Moral Crises: Magical and Secular Solutions' in *The Allocation of Responsibility* ed. Max Gluckman (Manchester, 1972) p. 6, where Evans Pritchard's views are also discussed. That what is called 'event causation' and 'agent causation' both seem to be present in the same situation is, as we shall see, not only a puzzle for 'primitives'.
5. For the background of the notion of αἰτία as bearing an imputation of guilt and responsibility, and the carrying over of this into its causal use, see G. Lloyd, *Magic, Reason and Experience* (Cambridge, 1979) pp. 49 ff. Professor Lloyd has discussed the way in which certain other Greek causal terms carry over from social meanings – notably δύναμς as power, and ἀρχη as a principle, which was originally a source of authoritative rule. See his *Polarity and Analogy* (Cambridge, 1966) pp. 230 ff.
6. J. L. Austin, 'A Plea for Excuses', in *Philosophical Papers*, ed. J. O. Urmson and G. J. Warnock (Oxford, 1961) pp. 150–1.
7. Alan R. White, introduction to *The Philosophy of Action: Oxford Readings in Philosophy*, ed. Alan R. White (1968) p. 17. The 'rule' is that 'there is nothing in any object considered in itself which can afford us a reason for drawing a conclusion beyond it': *Treatise of Human Nature*, vol. 1, iii, 12. I shall be returning to the substance of this later; my present concern is simply to point out that it is called a rule.
8. Donald Davidson, 'Causal Relations', reprinted in *Essays on Actions and Events* (Oxford, 1981) p. 158.
9. D. H. Mellor, *Real Time* (Cambridge, 1981) p. 124. I shall be returning later to Mellor's view, and to other aspects of it.
10. J. L. Mackie, *The Cement of the Universe* (Oxford, 1974) p. 225. Hume's remark is at the end of the Abstract to the *Treatise of Human Nature*.
11. Richard Taylor, *Action and Purpose* (New Jersey, 1966) p. 39.

2 CAUSATION IN A ZENO UNIVERSE

1. I owe this last example to D. H. Mellor, *Real Time* (Cambridge, 1981) p. 119.
2. Samuel Taylor Coleridge, 'Frost at Midnight'. In the Preface to the *Lyrical Ballads* Wordsworth speaks of the 'goings-on' of the universe. I like this.
3. And, opprobriously, e.g. someone's lecture might be said to be a 'non-event'. I shall be suggesting that there may be non-events in a more philosophical sense.
4. It might be said that this would not apply in the kind of event ontology where everything is an event. But I shall be claiming later that even here there has to be some way of bounding an event, so as to say what it includes and what it excludes.
5. I say 'normally', as I do not want to beg the question over 'action at a distance'; this, however, is a matter of a spatial rather than of a temporal gap.
6. C. J. Ducasse, 'On the Nature and Observability of the Causal Relation', *Journal of Philosophy* (1926) no. 23. Reprinted in *Causation and Conditionals*, ed. E. Sosa (Oxford, 1975).
7. See Bertrand Russell, *Human Knowledge: Its Scope and Limits* (London, 1948) pp. 476 ff.
8. Bertrand Russell, *The Principles of Mathematics.* §§442–6; 2nd edn (London, 1937) pp. 469–73.
9. A. Michotte, *La Perception de le Causalité* (Lourain, 1946) Translated by T. R. Miles and E. Miles as *The Perception of Causality* (London, 1963).
10. T. R. Miles translates the French *entrainement* as 'entrainment', since this has a technical meaning he wants to preserve, though this is not a usual English word. The OED does indeed give a sense of 'to entrain' as 'to draw away with . . . oneself'. For Michotte the idea is that of carrying forward rather than drawing. Sir Frederic Bartlett is reported to have called it 'pushing with follow up'. *The Perception of Causality*, glossary, p. XV.
11. Ibid., p. 228. It should be noted that Michotte's experiments in the perception of causality are directed to visual, and not *kinaesthetic* sensations.
12. Of course the film has to be run through to get the succession, so an actual movement somewhere is needed to produce the illusion. But this is not what we see when we look at the film.
13. Kant, *Critique of Pure Reason*, Analogies of Experience: Second Analogy, A. 189 ff: B. 232 ff.
14. Ibid., A. 200: B. 246.
15. See e.g. A. C. Ewing, *Kant's Treatment of Causality* (London, 1924) pp. 86 ff. Ewing claims that Kant is saying that an objective sequence must necessarily be determined by some cause, and what this cause is may be discovered inductively. This is more than I find in the Second Analogy.
16. Schopenhauer, *The Fourfold Root of the Principle of Sufficient Reason*, ¶ 23, English translation by E. F. J. Payne (Illinois, 1974). See also Thomas Reid *Essays on the Active Powers of the Human Mind*, Essay IV (Edinburgh, 1788) ch. 9.
17. Kant deals with the problem of simultaneity, illustrated where a lead ball makes a depression in a cushion, by saying it is the *order* of time, not the *lapse* of time with which we have to reckon. 'If I lay the ball on the cushion, a

hollow follows upon the previous flat smooth shape; but if (for any reason) there previously exists a hollow in the cushion, a lead ball does not follow upon it', ibid., A. 203. B. 248. The priority can be shown by dependence in a conditional: 'if there is a depression in a cushion, there is a lead ball (or some other heavy object)', but not 'if there is a lead ball (or some other heavy object) there is a depression in a cushion'.

18. See Mellor, *Real Time*, ch. 10, 'Prediction, time travel and backward causation'. For a discussion of attempts to put a case for backward causation, see J. L. Mackie, 'The Cement of the Universe', pp. 162 ff (there is a note on the literature on p. 162). The *locus classicus* of this discussion was the symposium 'Can an Effect Precede its Cause?' between M. Dummett and A. Flew in the *Aristotelian Society*, supplementary vol. xxviii (1954).

19. In 'Fixed Past, Unfixed Future' to be published in *Contributions to Philosophy: Michael Dummett*, ed. Barry Taylor (The Hague) Mellor argues that, whereas chances (as objective probabilities) can be altered for a future occurrence by our actions now, chances of something having occurred in the past remain either 1 or 0 whatever we do now.

20. Introducing the revised 'De Quadratura Curvarum'. See *Mathematical Papers of Isaac Newton*, ed. D. T. Whiteside, vol. 8 (Cambridge, 1981) p. 107. I am grateful to Christopher Clarke for calling my attention to this passage and to E. McMullin for discussion.

21. A. Koyré has brought out this transition from 'physical' to 'mathematical' concepts. See his *Newtonian Studies* (Harvard, 1965), especially ch. 1 and appendix 1 'The State of Motion and the State of Rest', pp. 188 ff. I am indebted to Christopher Clarke for this reference also.

22. Quoted by A. Koyré, ibid., p. 150.

3 EVENTS AND NON-EVENTS

1. W. van O. Quine, *Word and Object* (New York and London, 1960) p. 171.
2. See Donald Davidson in *Actions and Events* (Oxford, 1981) pp. 124–5, and also in *The Logic of Decision and Action*, ed. N. Rescher (Pittsburgh, 1966) pp. 116–17.
3. W. v. O. Quine, *Ways of Paradox* (Harvard, 1976) p. 260.
4. E. J. Lemmon in *The Logic of Decision and Action*, pp. 96–103.
5. Ibid., p. 99. 'Jones buttered the toast with a knife in the bathroom at midnight' is Davidson's picturesque example of an event (see *Actions and Events*, p. 105).
6. See A. N. Whitehead, *The Concept of Nature* (Cambridge, 1920) p. 145; pp. 186–7.
7. This has become something of a stock example in the literature; to the best of my knowledge, it made its first appearance in William Kneale's paper 'Intentionality and Intensionality', *Aristotelian Society*, supplementary vol. 52, (1968).
8. See Jaegwon Kim, 'Events and their Descriptions' in *Essays in Honour of Carl G. Hempel*, ed. N. Rescher (Reidel, 1969); 'Causation, Nomic Subsumption, and the Concept of Event', *Journal of Philosophy*, vol. lxx

(1973) no. 8; also 'Events as Property Exemplifications' in *Action Theory*, ed. M. Brand and D. Walton (Reidel, 1976).

9. Kim also is prepared to say that the addition of what Davidson calls an 'adverbial modifier' will produce another event. Davidson avoids this by saying the adverbial modifiers can be detached. In Davidson's example of Sebastian taking a stroll in Bologna at 2 a.m. (see *Actions and Event*, p. 197), 'strolling' and 'strolling leisurely' for Kim would be two generic events with their constitutive properties. There are indefinitely many strolls that Sebastian could take. If he was strolling, and strolling leisurely, these would presumably be exemplifications of two generic events at the same time. There is something strongly counter-intuitive about a multiplication of descriptions producing a multiplication of events. (I shall have more to say of this in the next chapter.)

10. See especially Whitehead, *An Enquiry Concerning the Principles of Natural Knowledge* (Cambridge, 1919) p. 62 ff.

11. Mellor, *Real Time*, pp. 132–4.

12. 'Objects', that is, in the ordinary substantive sense, not in Whitehead's special sense, where they are 'adjectives' of events.

13. Mellor, 'In Defense of Dispositions', *Philosophical Review*. vol. LXXXIII (1974) no. 2, p. 173.

14. See Sidney Shoemaker, 'Identity, Properties, and Causality' in *Midwest Studies in Philosophy*, vol. IV (University of Minnesota, 1979) pp. 321 ff. and 'Causality and Properties' in *Time and Causation: Essays presented to Richard Taylor*, ed. Peter Van Imwagen (Reidal, 1980).

15. 'Cambridge changes' were so called because having different properties at different times was the definition of change given by Russell and also McTaggart in Cambridge; the name 'Cambridge changes' was coined by Peter Geach; see *God and the Soul* (Cambridge, 1969) p. 71.

16. Shoemaker, 'Identity, Properties and Causality' in *Midwest Studies in Philosophy*, vol. IV, p. 325.

17. Ibid., p. 335.

18. See Mellor's contribution to the discussion of Shoemaker's paper 'Properties, Causation and Projectibility', in *Applications of Inductive Logic*, ed. J. Cohen and Mary Hesse (Oxford, 1980).

4 EVENT CAUSATION

1. Bertrand Russell, *Problems of Philosophy* (London, 1912) p. 98. For 'animal induction', see *Human Knowledge: its Scope and Limits* (London, 1948) pp. 451–2.

2. For a defence of Hume's own views on this, see *Hume and the Problem of Causation* by Tom L. Beauchamp and Alexander Rosenberg (Oxford and New York, 1981). They bring out how, in his 'Rules by which to judge of causes and effects', Hume showed he was well aware of the need to have ways of distinguishing law-like and accidental generalities in speaking of causal sequences. He had a more sophisticated view than one of mere

induction by simple enumeration, though none the less one in which the causal connection itself is subjective; what is objective are observed regular successions.

3. R. B. Braithwaite, *Scientific Explanation* (Cambridge, 1953). See especially ch. 9, 'Laws of nature and causality'.
4. See W. E. Johnson, *Logic* (Cambridge, 1921) part 3, ch. 1.
5. *Science, Belief and Behaviour*, ed. D. H. Mellor (Cambridge, 1980).
6. For this view, see 'The Extensionality of Causal Contexts' by Alexander Rosenberg and Robert M. Martin, in *Midwest Studies in Philosophy*, vol. IV (1979) pp. 401 ff.
7. G. E. M. Anscombe, 'Causality and Extensionality', *Journal of Philosophy* vol. 66 (1969) p. 155.
8. For another statement of this, see 'The Causal Relation', by Peter Achinstein, *Midwest Studies in Philosophy*, vol. IV (1979) pp. 369 ff.
9. This would not, I think, be Miss Anscombe's way of putting the relevance of an aspect to a causal explanation, since she does not give this role to generalisations. See her inaugural lecture 'Causality and Determination', reprinted in *Causation and Conditionals*, ed. E. Sosa (Oxford, 1975).
10. Donald Davidson, 'Causal Relations' in *Actions and Events*, p. 162.
11. Ibid., p. 158.
12. Ibid., p. 156.
13. Beauchamp and Rosenberg, *Hume and the Problem of Causation*, pp. 270 ff.
14. Ibid., p. 274.
15. Davidson, 'The Logical Form of Action Sentences' in *Actions and Events*, pp. 105 ff.
16. This was pointed out by P. M. S. Hacker in 'Events, Ontology and Grammar', *Philosophy*, vol. 57 (Oct. 1982). The example is his.
17. Davidson, 'Causal Relations' in *Actions and Events*, p. 157.
18. Gerald Vision, *Mind*, vol. LXXXVII (1979) pp. 105 ff.
19. See Chapter 6.
20. L. J. O'Neill, *Mind*, vol. LXXXIX (1980) pp. 595 ff.
21. G. Vision, *Mind*, vol. XCI (1982) pp. 273 ff.
22. I shall be saying more later on how omissions (which in many cases state possibilities) can be given as causes indirectly through counterfactuals: if the captain had proceeded more cautiously, the disaster might not have happened. See pp. 60–1.
23. J. S. Mill, *A System of Logic*, book III, ch. v, § 3. Davidson refers to this passage in leading up to his example of Brutus stabbing Caesar. See *Actions and Events*, p. 156.
24. Karl Popper, *The Logic of Scientific Discovery* (London, 1959) part II, ch. 3, § 12, p. 59.
25. I shall be looking at this kind of explanation in Chapter 6.
26. Davidson, *Actions and Events*, p. 53.
27. G. H. von Wright, 'on the Logic and Epistemology of the Causal Relation' in *Logic, Methodology and Philosophy of Science*, IV, ed. P. Suppes *et al.* Reprinted in *Causation and Conditionals*, ed. E. Sosa, p. 113.
28. von Wright, *Explanation and Understanding* (London, 1971) p. 64.
29. Ibid., p. 82.
30. von Wright, *Causality and Determinism* (New York, 1974) p. 51.

31. R. G. Collingwood, *Proceedings of the Aristotelian Society* (1939) expanded as part III, section C of his *Essay on Metaphysics* (Oxford, 1940).
32. von Wright, *Causality and Determinism*, p. 49.
33. von Wright, *Explanation and Understanding*, p. 68.
34. Bertrand Russell, 'On the notion of Cause', *Proceedings of the Aristotelian Society* (1912). Reprinted in *Mysticism and Logic* (London, 1917).
35. This does not, of course, go for all who have recently written about causation. D. H. Mellor, for instance, in *Real Time* takes our actions as having effects as a paradigm instance.

5 ACTIONS

1. H. A. Prichard, in 'Acting, Willing and Desiring' in *The Philosophy of Action, Oxford Readings in Philosophy*, ed. Alan R. White (1968) p. 65.
2. Donald Davidson, 'Agency' in *Actions and Events* (Oxford, 1981) p. 59.
3. See Prichard's British Academy Lecture, 'Duty and Ignorance of Fact' (1932). Reprinted in *Moral Obligation* (Oxford, 1949).
4. See J. Feinberg, 'Action and Responsibility' in *Philosophy in America*, ed. M. Black (Cornell, 1965) p. 146.
5. Arthur Danto, in 'What we can do', *Journal of Philosophy*, LX (1963).
6. Danto, 'Basic Actions' *American Philosophical Quarterly*, vol. 2 (1965).
7. Cf. F. Stoutland, in 'Basic Actions and Causality', *Journal of Philosophy*, LXV (1968) p. 467, and J. Hornsby, *Actions* (London, 1980) pp. 70 ff.
8. Antoine de Saint-Exupéry, *Wind, Sand and Stars*, trans. by Lewis Galantière (London, 1970) pp. 73, 75–6.
9. Ibid., pp. 47–8.
10. Cf. G. Ryle, *The Concept of Mind* (London, 1949) esp. pp. 74 ff. 'To frown intentionally . . . is not to bring about a frown on one's forehead by first bringing about a frown-causing exertion of some occult non-muscle.'
11. Davidson, 'Agency', reprinted in *Actions and Events*, esp. p. 53.
12. Prichard, 'Duty and Ignorance of Fact', pp. 31–2. In a later paper, he withdrew this expression in favour of 'willing'. I do not think this is an improvement, for the reasons I have stated. Republished in *The Philosophy of Action*, ed. A. R. White.
13. J. Hornsby, *Actions*, p. 38.
14. Since I use the words 'intentional' and 'intensional' fairly often, I take this opportunity to underline the difference between them. 'Intentional' is used where an action is directed to an objective (and sometimes, more widely, following Brentano and Meinong, where a thought is directed to an object). This is a sub-class of the 'intensional', which is contrasted with 'extensional'. In extensionality, if x is identical with y, then everything true of x will be true of y, and any term substituted for another with the same reference will have the same truth values. In intensionality, expressions contain terms for mental states, and this means that substituted expressions with the same reference may not have the same truth values (this is a logical and not a psychological distinction). So 'Oedipus wished to kill the haughty stranger' is true, but 'Oedipus wished to kill his father' is not, although his father and the haughty stranger were the same person.

15. Hornsby, *Actions*, p. 38.
16. See especially Davidson's paper 'Agency' in *Actions and Events*. The passage quoted is on p. 53.
17. See on this J. L. Austin, 'A Plea for Excuses', reprinted in *Philosophical Papers*, ed. J. O. Urmson and G. J. Warnock (Oxford, 1961).
18. G. E. M. Anscombe, *Intention*, (Oxford, 1957).
19. 'Under a description', reprinted in *The Collected Philosophical Papers of G. E. M. Anscombe*, vol. II (Oxford, 1981) pp. 208 ff, from *Nous*, no. XIII (1979).

6 CAUSES AS SELECT FACTORS

1. J. S. Mill, *A System of Logic*, book III, ch. 5, 5.3.
2. P. Bridgman, *The Logic of Modern Physics* (New York, 1928) p. 83. I owe the quotation to N. Hanson, *Patterns of Discovery* (Cambridge, 1958) p. 50.
3. An extreme version of this is the kind of idealism which makes the whole universe into a single system of internal relations, and then calls these causal, so that it is said that everything is directly or indirectly causally related to everything else. Cf. Brand Blanshard, *The Nature of Thought*, vol. 2 (London 1939) p. 492.
4. R. G. Collingwood, *Essay on Metaphysics* (Oxford, 1940) pp. 285 ff.
5. This is in effect Davidson's view of reasons as causes in 'Actions, Reasons and Causes' in *Journal of Philosophy* no. LX (1963) pp. 685–700. Republished in *Actions and Events* (Oxford, 1981).
6. See pp. 38–9.
7. See Raymond Martin, 'Singular Causal Explanation' in *Theory and Decision*, no. II (1972). I owe the reference to Bart Gruzalski's discussion piece 'Killing and Letting Die' in *Mind*, XC (1981) pp. 94 ff. Gruzalski uses this view to mark the differentiating factor in a medical context between patients with pneumonia treated with an antibiotic and a patient not so treated who dies, and he says that it would be proper to cite the failure to give the antibiotic as the cause of death, thereby making the act of letting die count as an act of killing. In such cases, where 'cause' is used to mean 'responsible for', acts of omission can be causes. They satisfy counter-factuals: if the patient had been given the antibiotic, he would (might?) not have died. (I think this is harsh on the doctors if the antibiotic was still being tested. If it was known to be effective, they might be said to have been negligent.)
8. BBC Radio, 13 February 1981.
9. See 'Causes and Conditions' reprinted from *The American Philosophical Quarterly in Causation and Conditionals*, ed. E. Sosa.
10. J. L. Mackie, *The Cement of the Universe* (Oxford, 1974) p. 35.
11. M. Bunzl, 'Causal Overdetermination', *Journal of Philosophy*, no. LXXVI (1979) pp. 134 ff.
12. H. L. A. Hart and A. M. Honoré, *Causation in the Law* (Oxford, 1959).
13. Law Reports, *The Times*, 17 May 1981.
14. Recalling the ambiguity in the Greek word αἰτία.

15. This may be denied by Miss Anscombe, who treats with scorn appeals to general regularities in talking about causation. She thinks the notion has a sufficient lodging in a language which contains words like 'scrape', 'push', 'knock over'. See her 'Causality and Determinism', Inaugural Lecture, Cambridge 1971. Reprinted in *Causation and Conditionals*, ed. E. Sosa, pp. 63 ff.
16. The expressions 'nomic necessity' and 'universals of fact' come originally from W. E. Johnson, *Logic*, part 3, ch. 1 (Cambridge, 1921).
17. Cf. on this R. B. Braithwaite, *Scientific Explanation*, ch. 9.

7 MULTIPLE CAUSES AND THE MULTIPLICITY OF 'CAUSE'

1. Montesquieu, *Esprit des Lois*, book xiv, ch. 13.
2. Max Weber, *Die Protestantiche Ethik und der Geist des Kapitalismus*, trans. as *The Protestant Ethic* (London, 1930).
3. R. H. Tawney, *Religion and the Rise of Capitalism* (London, 1926).
4. W. H. Dray, *Laws and Explanations in History* (Oxford, 1957). See esp. ch. 6, 8, 3, on 'How possibly' explanations.
5. *Animal Behaviour*, vol. 3 (1983) pp. 52–81, ed. T. R. Halliday and P. J. B. Slater.
6. I have noted that even Mackie's definition of an INUS factor (an insufficient but necessary part of a condition which is unnecessary but sufficient) need not give a unique factor as cause.
7. Zeno Vendler, 'Causal Relations', *Journal of Philosophy*, no. lxiv (1967) p. 704, and also his paper in the Symposium, 'Effects, Results and Consequences' in *Analytical Philosophy*, first series, ed R. J. Butler (Oxford, 1966).
8. Experimental science is concerned with diagnosing relevant distinct factors. Where this has not been developed, there are other ways in which people try to single out some factors from the whole web of interconnections. Joseph Needham reports how in Ancient China these were 'intuited analogical correspondences in the repertory of correlations'. *Science and Civilization in China*, vol. 2 (Cambridge, 1955) p. 290.
9. See P. Winch, *The Idea of a Social Science* (London, 1958).
10. Nigel Walker, 'Unscientific, Unwise, Unprofitable or Unjust?', *British Journal of Criminology,* vol. 22 (July, 1982) p. 278.
11. Nigel Walker, *Behaviour and Misbehaviour: explanations and non-explanations* (Oxford, 1977).
12. Ian Taylor, Paul Walton and Jock Young, *The New Criminology* (London, 1973). See Walker, *Behaviour and Misbehaviour*, pp. 26 ff.
13. Walker, *Behaviour and Misbehaviour*, p. 133. The quotation is from E. Glover, *The Roots of Crime: Selected Papers on Psycho-Analysis* (New York, 1964) p. 302.
14. John Watson, *Which is the Justice? Reflections of a juvenile court magistrate* (London, 1969) pp. 138–9.
15. Ibid., p. 112.

16. There is a most helpful discussion of this by William Charlton in his commentary on his translation of Aristotle's *Physics* I and II (Oxford, 1970). See esp. pp. 98 ff., commenting on II iii.
17. Richard Sorabji brings this out in his *Necessity, Cause and Blame* (London, 1980). See especially ch. 2.
18. Aristotle, *Physics* II, iii, 194b, 9. W. H. Charlton translates ἠρεμήσεως 'Staying Unchanged'. My attention was called to this passage by Richard Sorabji.
19. Ibid., 195a, 12.
20. This is stated explicitly in Aristotle's *Metaphysics* i, 1013a, where different meanings of 'cause', αἰτία are connected with different meanings of 'principle', ἀρχή.

8 IMMANENT AND TRANSEUNT CAUSATION

1. See Roderick Chisholm, 'Freedom and Action', in *Freedom and Determinism*, ed. K. Lehrer (New York, 1966).
2. Aristotle, *Metaphysics*, 1050a, 30–5.
3. St Thomas Aquinas, *Summa Theologica* II i, *quaestio* 57, art. 4.
4. Chisholm, 'Freedom and Action', in *Freedom and Determinism*, p. 18. Chisholm quotes Aristotle, *Physics* VII 5, 256 a, 6–8: 'Thus a staff moves a stone and is moved by a hand, which is moved by a man.' This differs from the distinction in *Metaphysics* 1050a 30, which was the one the mediaevals took up.
5. Von Wright, *Explanation and Understanding* (Ithaca, 1972) pp. 191–2.
6. See W. E. Johnson's *Logic* (Cambridge, 1921) vol. III, especially the introduction, pp. xxiii–v, and ch. 9. Note that Johnson uses the old spelling 'transeunt', not 'transient'. 'Transeunt' was used in the 17th century, in speaking of causation as 'passing from the doer to that which is done', and was contrasted with 'immanent' (OED).
7. Ibid., part III, pp. 128 ff.
8. Ibid., part II, 98–9. The term 'functionally' may be important, and I shall be returning to it.
9. See D. H. Mellor, *Real Time* (Cambridge, 1981) pp. 126–7.
10. J. L. Mackie, *The Cement of the Universe* (Oxford, 1974) p. 154.
11. Ibid., p. 225, his italics. On pp. 156–9 he says that the notion of causation should be extended to cover the earlier phases of persisting objects and self-maintaining processes, calling this 'immanent causation'.
12. David Wiggins, *Sameness and Substance* (Oxford, 1980).
13. This is discussed by Vernon Pratt, in an article 'Biological Classification', *British Journal for the Philosophy of Science*, vol. 23 (1972). Pratt defends classifications of organisms into groups in a fundamental way which will support inductive inferences, and he holds that the most promising distinction is that of phylogenetically based groups with similar genetic endowment.
14. Wiggins, *Sameness and Substance*, p. 80.
15. Hobbes uses this example, originally Plutarch's. See Wiggins, ibid., p. 92 ff.

16. I have not looked at what makes for identity in the particular kinds of artifact we call institutions. This would combine function with procedures and practices which can be more and less explicitly formulated. How far an institution can be said to be the same while its members and participants pass through it and pass on, and where it may have had periods in which it is closed or not in session, will depend, I think, on *some* specifiable function and procedures. These may change over time. There can be continuity in the institution where procedures for change have been followed with some regard to the function as interpreted at the time. All this is an interesting matter; it has indeed often been discussed by sociologists and lawyers. For my present concern, the kind of identity found in institutions will depend on how their participants act, and on how they think it is proper for them to act.

17. See A. N. Whitehead, *Process and Reality* (Cambridge, 1929; New York, 1929; New York, 1978) p. 48, p. 53, p. 35 respectively. Also 'Time', *Sixth International Congress of Philosophy* (Harvard, 1926) p. 64. I am not drawing on Whitehead's later conception of 'prehensions', which is a 'picking up' rather than a 'passing on' view of causation. I find it very hard to see how a supervening entity 'conforms' to an earlier one by appropriating its 'feelings' when the latter has perished. But that is another story. (I have tried to look at it in a paper 'Whitehead's view of Causal Efficacy' in the Proceedings of the International Symposium 'Whiteheads und der Prozessbegiff' ('Whitehead and the Idea of Process') in Bonn in 1981 to be published by Verlag Karl Alber (Freiburg) in 1984. I am more sympathetic to the earlier view of the 'passage of nature' which suggests that the conformation of a later to an earlier stage comes from the character of the process as an on-going activity. I was helped in thinking about this by some at present unpublished discussions on Whitehead among the Epiphany Philosophers.

18. See A. N. Whitehead, *Essays in Science and Philosophy* (New York, 1947) p. 117.

19. A. N. Whitehead, *The Concept of Nature* (Cambridge, 1926) p. 143.

20. Dorothy Emmet, *Whitehead's Philosophy of Organism* (London, 1932).

21. This is where I part company with R. Harré and E. M. Madden in their *Causal Powers. A Theory of Natural Necessity* (Oxford, 1975). Harré and Madden do indeed try to show that the 'natures' are more than formal by saying that science may discover the *modus operandi* of their causal powers. I agree with them in wanting a realist view of causal operations, but I should not want to call this natural necessity.

22. And I agree with Mellor that the hypothetical sense is not sufficient even for dispositions.

9 IMMANENT CAUSATION IN MEMORY

1. *Collected Letters of Samuel Taylor Coleridge*, ed. E. L. Griggs (Oxford, 1971) vol. 5, no. 1325, p. 266. There is undoubtedly a reference here to the 'Brocken spectre', the shadow of a man cast by the rays of the rising or setting sun on to a bank of mist, so that he sees what appears to be a giant figure whose head is surrounded by rings of light called 'glories'. See the end

of 'Constancy to an Ideal Object', and Stephen Prickett, *Wordsworth and Coleridge* (Cambridge, 1970) p. 22, for how Coleridge frequently reverted to this image.

2. Richard Wollheim, 'Memory, Experiential Memory, and Personal Identity', in *Perception and Identity. Essays presented to A. J. Ayer*, ed. G. F. Macdonald (London, 1979). The quotation is from p. 224.

3. Bertrand Russell, *The Analysis of Mind* (London, 1921) p. 78.

4. Here F. Bartlett's *Remembering: A study in experimental and social psychology* (Cambridge, 1932) is still a classic. H. A. Bursen, *Dismantling the Memory Machine* (Reidel, 1978) has a devastating attack on 'trace' theories.

5. In *Matière et Memoire*, trans. as *Matter and Memory* (London, 1911), Bergson is very good on the difference between habit memory that can become a bodily set, and recollection.

6. The classical expression of this is, of course, Proust's *A la récherche du temps perdu*.

7. I owe this example to Professor Charles Hartshorne.

8. B. F. Skinner, *The Behaviour of Organisms* (New York, 1938) pp. 7–8. See M. Midgley, *Beast and Man* (Brighton, 1978) p. 109.

9. This has been described and illustrated by Merleau-Ponty in *La structure du comportement* (Paris, 1942).

10. Rainer Maria Rilke, *Gesammelte Werke* vol. ı (Leipzig, 1927) pp. 360–3. I am grateful to Peter Stern for helping me with the translation.

11. More of this in the next chapter.

10 IMMANENT CAUSATION IN ORGANISMS AND IN BODY–MIND

1. See especially E. Rignano, *Biological Memory*, trans. E. W. MacBride (London, 1926), where it is suggested this is accumulated in a special store of nervous energy at the centre. (The phenomenon, however, occurs in organism such as sponges which do not have a nervous system.) Rignano was, of course, writing before the development of modern genetics. But genetics does not fully answer the problem to which he called attention.

2. A. N. Whitehead, *Science and the Modern World* (Cambridge, 1926) p. 112.

3. A. N. Whitehead, *An Enquiry into the Principles of Natural Knowledge* (Cambridge, 1919) p. 3.

4. See A. N. Whitehead, 'Time, Space and the Material', *Proceedings of the Aristotelian Society* (1922–3) esp. ch. 8.

5. A. N. Whitehead, *Principles of Natural Knowledge*, p. 167.

6. In the chapter 'The Quantum Theory' in *Science and the Modern World*, Whitehead saw support for this in Quantum Theory as he knew it (*c.* 1924) where electro-magnetic energy was shown to be emitted and absorbed in quanta. He was not taking account of the new quantum theory of Schrödinger, Heisenberg, and others which was currently being produced; there is no probabilistic theory in his view, nor anything answering to the Heisenberg uncertainty principle. So analogies between Whitehead's views and modern quantum theory need to be treated with caution. A. Shimony,

'Quantum Physics and the Philosophy of Whitehead' in *Boston Studies in the Philosophy of Science* vol. ii (1965) has called attention to some of these differences. (He suggests that an analogy can be found by developing a later Whiteheadian view of 'fields of feelings'; this terminology seems to me very implausible.)

7. There are of course other distinctions in living organisms, notably searching behaviour in finding adaptations, so that they show not only repetition of patterns, but the establishing of new ones. This, however, goes beyond my present concern.

8. A. R. Sheldrake, *A New Science of Life: The Hypothesis of Formative Causation* (London, 1981).

9. There is a vast literature on this. In the 1950s, the main view was put by L. Bertalanffy in *Problems of Life* (London, 1952). He has an extensive bibliography. For a more recent presentation, see Paul A. Weiss, 'The living system: determinism stratified', in *Beyond Reductionism*, ed. A. Koestler and J. R. Smythies (London, 1969).

10. Whitehead, *Principles of Natural Knowledge*, p. 3.

11. There are of course, versions of the 'Argument to Design' which see organisms in that way, for instance Paley, in his 'Evidences of the Existence and Attributes of the Deity Collected from the Appearances of Nature' in *Natural Theology* (London, 1802). But such views do not pinpoint the functioning of organisms in self-maintenance; they see them as contrived machines.

12. I tried to look at this in more detail in my book *Function, Purpose and Powers* (London, 1958) where I was especially concerned with confusions between the two kinds of teleology in functional sociology.

13. Paul A. Weiss, 'The living system: determinism stratified', in *Beyond Reductionism*, ed. Koestler and Smythies.

14. C. S. Peirce, *Collected Papers*, 6.101, ed. Hartshorne and Weiss (Harvard, 1935).

15. Ibid., 6.300.

16. Barbara Brown, *New Mind, New Body* (London, 1975) p. 75.

17. Kathleen Wilkes, *Physicalism*, in the series *Studies in Philosophical Psychology* (London, 1979).

18. Robert Kirk, 'From Physical Explicability to Full-Bodied Materialism', *Philosophical Quarterly*, vol. 29 (July, 1979).

19. Austin Farrer, *The Freedom of the Will* (London, 1958) p. 24.

20. 'Intelligent' here, of course, means what is sometimes called 'goal directed'. It does not mean doing what is a sensible thing to do, which it may or may not be.

21. This is the formulation given by C. D. Broad in *Mind and its Place in Nature* (London, 1925) p. 61. On the whole, Broad himself favours 'Emergent Materialism' as the most plausible of the theories of 'Mind and Matter', of which he lists seventeen on pp. 608–11.

22. This 'play back' distinguishes this kind of emergence view from epiphenomenalism, or the view of the mental as supervenient.

23. Gilbert Ryle, *The Concept of Mind* (London, 1949) p. 16.

11 EFFICACIOUS GRACE

1. J. R. Illingworth, *Divine Immanence* (London, 1898).
2. Helen Oppenheimer, *Immanence and Incarnation* (London, 1973) ch. 12.
3. A. C. Ewing, *Idealism* (London, 1934) ch. 4.
4. William James tells how, when a New England child was told that God 'is everywhere about us: He pervades', the child said: 'Oh then, He is a skunk.' How could the word 'pervade' suggest anything else to an American child? *The Thought and Character of William James*, ed. R. B. Perry, vol. 2 (Boston, 1936) p. 358.
5. F. H. Bradley, 'On God and the Absolute', *Essays on Truth and Reality* (Oxford, 1914) p. 437.
6. John Laird, *Mind and Deity* (London, 1941) p. 269.
7. Ibid., p. 288.
8. Austin Farrer, *Faith and Speculation* (London, 1967) p. 150.
9. Margaret Masterman, 'The Psychology of Levels of Will', *Proceedings of the Aristotelian Society*, vol. XLVIII (1946–7).
10. Dorothy Emmet, *The Moral Prism* (London, 1979) especially ch. 7.

Index

134 *Index*